MARBLE MANIA®

Edited by Stanley A. Block

Revised & Expanded
2nd Edition

4880 Lower Valley Rd. Atglen, PA 19310 USA

This book is dedicated to my family, from whom the hobby has taken so much time, and to all the youngsters who have played marbles; many are today's collectors.

Other Schiffer Books on Related Subjects:
Marble Collectors Handbook. Robert Block. ISBN:0-7643-2331-8. $16.95
Marbles Identification and Price Guide. Robert Block. ISBN:0-7643-1574-9. $19.95.
Popular American Marbles. Dean Six. ISBN:0-7643-2640-0. $14.95
Contemporary Marbles,& Related Art Glass. Mark P. Block. ISBN: 0-7643-1166-2. $59.95
The Encyclopedia of Modern Marbles, Spheres and Orbs. Mark P. Block. ISBN: 0-7643-2294-X. $69.95

Revised price guide: 2010
Copyright © 1998 & 2010 by Stanley A. Block
Library of Congress Control Number: 2010940487

Design modified by Mark David Bowyer
Type set in Franklin Gothic ITC Hv BT / Garamond

ISBN: 978-0-7643-3550-1
Printed in China

Schiffer Books are available at special discounts for bulk purchases for sales promotions or premiums. Special editions, including personalized covers, corporate imprints, and excerpts can be created in large quantities for special needs. For more information contact the publisher:

Published by Schiffer Publishing Ltd.
4880 Lower Valley Road
Atglen, PA 19310
Phone: (610) 593-1777; Fax: (610) 593-2002
E-mail: Info@schifferbooks.com

For the largest selection of fine reference books on this and related subjects, please visit our web site at
www.schifferbooks.com
We are always looking for people to write books on new and related subjects. If you have an idea for a book please contact us at the above address.

This book may be purchased from the publisher.
Include $5.00 for shipping.
Please try your bookstore first.
You may write for a free catalog.

In Europe, Schiffer books are distributed by
Bushwood Books
6 Marksbury Ave.
Kew Gardens
Surrey TW9 4JF England
Phone: 44 (0) 20 8392 8585; Fax: 44 (0) 20 8392 9876
E-mail: info@bushwoodbooks.co.uk
Website: www.bushwoodbooks.co.uk

CONTENTS

ACKNOWLEDGMENTS

My sincere thanks go to all who have helped to make the Marble Collectors' Society of America and the hobby of marbles such a huge success. The hobby of marbles had taken its place in the field of sports, and now in the fields of antiques and collectibles. National tournaments have taken place in the United States since 1922 and in England since the late 1400s. In particular, I would like to thank those who have kept us informed of current events, have helped with articles, and have provided copies of printed materials and various marbles to aid the Society's library and collection programs.

I thank the contributing editors to this work and everyone whose efforts have made it a complete and meaningful part of the hobby. I am sure this book will help to promote the hobby and preserve some of the information known to date for future generations.

I would be remiss if I did not thank my family for undue hardships caused by my time spent for the Society and its projects. Also, I thank Bob and Mark for their help in preparing this revised edition.

Stanley A. Block

INTRODUCTION

This work is published as both a photographic gallery of marbles and a manual of known marble information. It is a compilation of information written by knowledgeable collectors who acted as contributing editors to this project. Each is a collector whose specialty is covered by the chapter authored.

This book is not intended to be a textbook, but rather a photographic manual of the hobby of marble collecting and marble memorabilia.

As can be seen from the Contents list, this book covers various aspects of the subject of marbles and is divided into six main sections: various non-glass marble types, early handmade glass, machine-made glass, contemporary handmade glass, games and toys, other uses.

Each of these sections could use additional research to make it as complete as possible and to keep it current. Books could be written, and in some cases have been written, on each one of the sections in this work.

Little is known about the history and production of antique marbles. Research to date has had little success in identifying the makers and production of antique marbles.

More is known and therefore published on marbles made in the United States. The sections and chapters follow the chronological order of marble making, even though there may be an overlapping of production periods. That is, clay, pottery, etc., continued in production after handmade glass marbles were first produced.

Since there is available information on both machine made and contemporary makers, the authors have, whenever possible, identified by maker the various marbles pictured. For example, many makers produced and still make clearies, while only one company made the original comic strip marbles.

Also, the works of art by contemporary craftsmen are attributable to each maker, and therefore are pictured that way. We have tried to cover most contemporary glass artists who have previously made or are now making marbles. Although this information is as complete as possible when we started this project, new artisans are trying new ideas every day.

The hobby of marbles is still in its infancy. A great deal of information and history still needs to be researched and pieced together. It is our hope this book will generate interest in all facets of the hobby.

Unless otherwise noted, all photos are from the collection of Stanley A. Block.

PRICES SHOWN

Four factors determine the value of a marble: type, size, condition, and eye appeal. Values shown in this book are for mint condition marbles in the average sizes for each category. Group photos are valued either individually or in total for the marbles shown, as noted. For comprehensive pricing of specific examples, we recommend consulting the most recent edition of The Society Price Guide, *Marbles: Identification and Price Guide* by Robert Block (Schiffer Publishing, 1998), 4th edition, 2002.

It is important to note that the prices shown for each photo are representative prices shown for that type of marble in mint condition, in the most common size. The actual marbles shown may be much larger or smaller and therefore have a greater or lesser value than shown.

Over the past twenty years, the popularity of various types of marbles has changed. During the 1990s, machine-made marbles were the hot category and during the last ten years contemporary artists' marbles were in vogue. At this time, the three categories (antique glass, machine-made and contemporary art glass) are about equal in collector desirability.

As each category grew in stature, prices of the other categories suffered. Pricing also slipped after the 9/11 tragedy and continued to fall during the recent recession. At the present time, autumn of 2010, we are beginning to see some growth in each of the categories. It is important to note that during the past decade of declining prices, marbles that are in mint condition or are rare have held their values.

The terminology "too rare to value," as used in this book, may mean the item referred to is extremely rare or one of a kind or we have no knowledge of there being any sale of the item to be a guide to the present value.

MARBLE COLLECTORS SOCIETY OF AMERICA

The marble Collectors Society of America was founded in 1975 as a non-profit organization established for charitable, scientific, literary, and educational purposes. The Society's objectives are to gather and disseminate information and perform services to further the hobby of marbles, marble collecting, and the preservation of the history of marbles and marble making. The Society currently has over 2,000 contributors.

Society projects include the quarterly newsletter, *Marble Mania*, color marble photograph plates, a videotape series, and contributors listing. In addition, they are in the process of ongoing research and the development of a collection of marbles for the Society library.

Other major accomplishments of the Society are various surveys; photographing and publishing color sheets; gathering and placing collections in the Smithsonian Institution, The Corning Museum of Glass, and the Wheaton Village Museum; publication of price guides and their periodic updates; preparation of slide presentations and contributor listings; and the research and issuance of articles concerning marble factories and contemporary marble makers.

Section I:

MARBLES—STONE, MINERAL, CLAY, POTTERY, PORCELAIN, AND CHINA

by Jeff Carskadden, Richard Gartley, and Others

STONE AND MINERAL

Stone and mineral marbles can be as varied and diverse as the number of types and colors of stones and minerals available. They were first used as toy marbles by youths who found the rounded stones alongside streams, where they had been tumbled to almost perfect spheres.

The most collectible of the mineral marbles were hand-cut and milled in Germany and Austria in the late 1800s and early 1900s. Idar Oberstein, Germany, is the most famous of the mineral cutting areas, and a huge cottage industry cut the agate cubes for milling in large water powered grinding mills. The agate marbles were hand polished on large wheels for export all over the world. The United States was a major importer, and many mail order catalogues of the era carry drawings and descriptions of the banded and dyed agates that are now so collectible. The dyed agates have beautiful shades of blue, green, black, and yellow. Many other items were also made from both the natural and dyed agates.

Other minerals and stones were used to make marbles, including those on the following list. Photographs of the materials indicated by an asterisk (*) can be found in the author's book *Marbles Beyond Glass*.

Marbles out of stone and minerals are still being produced today. However, they are now made in modern sphere-making machines and polished to a high gloss in commercial tumbling operations though some are still made by hand by a few craftsmen.

One way to distinguish early stone and mineral marbles from newer ones is by turning a marble slowly under a light source. Earlier marbles usually have at least one facet that will show itself under this method. Although a finely hand-polished early agate may be totally polished, you can usually find one facet or ridge to indicate the era it was produced in, although the mineral in most cases is thousands of years old.

Also classified in this group is a manmade mineral type called goldstone. It is usually a brown or blue material with thousands of uniform sparkles, and has been used in marbles and costume jewelry for nearly 100 years. Larger varieties of mineral marbles over 1-1/2 inches are usually called mineral spheres.

Agate, Banded *	Goldstone*	Quartz, Optical*
Agate, Carnelian*	Granite*	Quartz, Rose*
Agate, Lace*	Hematite	Quartz, Rutilated*
Agate, Picture	Holmquisite	Quartz, Smoky*
Amazonite	Howlite*	Rhodenite*
Amber	Illmenite	Rhodochrosite*
Amethyst*	Jade*	Richtorite
Ametrine	Jasper*	Ruby*
Ammonite	Jet	Sapphire*
Angelite*	Labradorite	Sardonyx
Anhydrite	Lapis Lazuli*	Scorzalite
Apatite	Lazurite	Selenite
Aquamarine	Leopardskin*	Septarian
Aragonite*	Limestone	Seraphenite
Astrophillite	Lodolite	Serpentine*
Aventurine*	Magnesite	Sphalerite
Azurite	Malachite*	Sodalite*
Bloodstone*	Marble	Stromatolite*
Brazilianite	Mariposite	Sugulite
Bustamite	Meteorite	Sunstone
Calcite	Moldavite	Thulite
Chalcopyrite	Mookaite	Tiger Iron*
Charoite	Moonstone	Tigereye, Blue*
Chert*	Morganite	Tigereye, Golden*
Christalite	Obicular*	Tigereye, Red*
Chrysocolla*	Obsidian*	Topaz
Chrysoprase	Olivine	Tourmaline
Citrine	Onyx*	Triphylite
Copper	Opal*	Turquoise
Coral	Opalite	Unikite
Damoltierite	Pectolite	Variscite*
Eudialite	Petrified Palm*	Whillolkite*
Fluorite*	Pietersite	Wolfeite*
Fuschite	Porphry*	Yekem*
Galena	Prehenite	
Garnet	Pyrite	

Group of Natural and Dyed Agate. $2,000-$3,000.

Natural Agate. $20-$30.

Natural Banded Agate. $25-$40.

Natural Agate. $15-$25.

Natural Banded Agate. $30-$50.

Natural Banded Agate. $20-$30.

Dyed Black Natural Banded Agate. $50-$75.

Natural Banded Agate. $25-$40.

Dyed Black Natural Banded Agate. $50-$75.

Natural Banded Agate. $25-$40.

Dyed Yellow Natural Banded Agate. $100-$150.

Natural Banded Agate. $25-$40.

Dyed Blue Natural Banded Agate. $75-$125.

Dyed Blue Natural
Banded Agate. $75-$125.

Dyed Green Natural
Banded Agate. $75-$125.

Dyed Green Natural
Banded Agate. $75-$125.

Dyed Blue Natural
Banded Agate. $75-$125.

Dyed Blue Natural
Banded Agate. $75-$125.

Dyed Blue Natural Banded
Agate. $100-$150.

Dyed Blue Natural Banded
Agate. $100-$150.

Dyed Green Natural
Banded Agate. $100-$150.

Group of Other Minerals. $700-$1,000.

Petrified wood. $30-$50.

Leopardskin. $30-$50.

Goldstone. $20-$35.

Golden Tigereye.
$20-$35.

Tiger Iron. $25-$40.

Red Tigereye. $25-$40.

Jasper with Quartz.
$20-$35.

Rose Quartz. $20-$35.

Green Aventurine.
$20-$35.

Flourite. $20-$35.

Turquoise. $20-$35.

Petrified Palmwood.
$20-$35.

Petrified Palmwood.
$20-$35.

Rhodenite. $20-$35.

Blue Lace Agate.
$20-$35.

Rutilated Quartz.
$20-$35.

Picture Agate. $20-$35.

Leopardskin. $30-$50.

Lapis Lazuli.
$20-$35.

CLAY, POTTERY, AND CROCKERY

Clay, pottery, and crockery type marbles have been commercially produced by the billions in Germany and the United States. These types were relatively inexpensive and easy to produce. Some have even been found in Egyptian tombs.

The first marble related patents issued in the United States were for devices that produced clay marbles in groups. **Clays** are the most common type. Old mail order catalogues refer to both German and United States types, which sold in boxes of 100 and mesh bags of 1,000.

Natural clay colors are browns and grays, however a great many clays were dyed, and can readily be found in red, blue, green, yellow, brown, and mottled colors.

Crockery, lined crockery, and **stoneware** marbles were also listed in many early mail order catalogues. It is presumed that many potteries in both Germany and the United States produced huge quantities of these marbles. These types were whiter and denser than clays. Some came with a glaze baked on, and as with clays, most were relatively inexpensive.

Bennington Marbles are a type of dyed and glazed pottery. The name is derived from their look-a-like appearance to pottery made at the Bennington Pottery in Bennington, Vermont. That pottery has no record of ever having produced marbles commercially. In addition, early catalogues list this type as imported. There are a number of original boxes surviving that have "Made in Germany" stamped on them. Some of these original boxes are also marked "Agates-Imitation Made in Germany."

The most plentiful type of Benningtons are brown or blue, and some are shades of green, white, yellow, or black. There are also "fancy" Benningtons which have a combination of blues, browns, and greens over a white base. The most difficult type of "fancy" Bennington to find has a red or pink base color instead of white. Benningtons are easier recognized by their "eyes." These eyes are spots on the marbles that were left when the marbles touched others during the firing of the glaze.

Crockery, lined crockery, and **stoneware** types were made in much smaller quantities and are more difficult to find. **Spongeware** is a stoneware type that is now sought after. They are usually over 1 inch in diameter, with sponged designs in blue, then salt glazed and fired.

Group of Clays. $3-$5.

Group of Clays.
$8-$15. *Collection of Anonymous.*

Group of Pottery and Crockery. $200-$300.

Lined Crockery.
$5-$8.

Lined Crockery.
$5-$8.

Lined Crockery.
$10-$15.

Lined Crockery.
$5-$8.

Lined Crockery.
$5-$8.

Lined Crockery.
$5-$8.

Lined Crockery.
$5-$8.

Lined Crockery.
$10-$15.

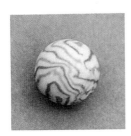

Lined Crockery.
$10-$15.

Lined Crockery.
$5-$8.

Sponge Ware. $60-$100.
Collection of Anonymous.

Sponge Ware. $75-$125.
Collection of Jeff Yale.

Sponge Ware. $60-$100.
*Collection of Trudy and Andy
Christian.*

Sponge Ware.
$30-$50.

Sponge Ware.
$15-$25.

Dyed Pottery. $10-$15.

Dyed Pottery. $15-$25.

Dyed Pottery. $5-$8.

Dyed Pottery. $5-$8.

Dyed Pottery. $5-$8.

Dyed Pottery. $5-$8.

Glazed White Ballot Box
Marble. 50¢-$1.

Glazed Black Ballot
Box Marble. 50¢-$1.

Brown 50¢
Bennington Type
Pottery. 50¢-$1.

Pink Base Fancy
Bennington Type
Pottery. $50-$75.

Pink Base Fancy
Bennington Type
Pottery. $50-$75.
*Collection of
Anonymous.*

Pink Base Fancy
Bennington Type
Pottery. $50-$75.
*Collection of Anony-
mous.*

Brown Bennington
Type Pottery. 50¢-$1.

Blue Bennington
Type Pottery.
75¢-$1.25.

Brown Bennington
Type Pottery. 50¢-$1.

Blue Bennington Type
Pottery. 75¢-$1.25.

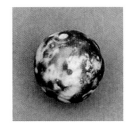

Green Bennington
Type Pottery. $10-$15.

Fancy Bennington
Type Pottery. $5-$8.

Fancy Bennington
Type Pottery. $5-$8.

Green Bennington
Type Pottery. $10-$15.

Fancy Bennington Type
Pottery. $5-$8. *Collec-
tion of Anonymous.*

Fancy Bennington
Type Pottery. $5-$8.

Blue and Brown Rare
Bennington Type
Pottery. $50-$75.

CHINA AND PORCELAIN

Starting in the mid-1840s, and continuing through the first decade of the 20th century, German toy makers fashioned marbles from porcelain and decorated these otherwise white marbles with hand-painted designs, including geometric patterns and flowers. Hand-painting was a popular form of decorating ceramic items in the 1840s, such as inexpensive porcelain tableware and decorative items, and German ceramic marble makers may have simply been following this general decorative trend. However, it may not have been a coincidence that the hand-painting of China marbles began about the same time that colorful handmade glass marbles were introduced by German toy makers. It could well be that the introduction of these new glass marbles forced the German ceramic marble makers to enhance their product line by adding hand-painted decorations to their China marbles.

Depending on the style and complexity of the designs and the presence or absence of a glazed surface, China marbles can be categorized into one of three general time periods that divide the seventy year span during which these marbles were popular. These time periods, discussed in more detail below, have been determined by examining China marbles found in archeological excavations.

Early or Civil War Period (ca. 1840-1870)

Most Chinas made during this period were unglazed, and their designs were painted over an unglazed surface. Although geometric designs such as intersecting sets of parallel lines were the most common motif seen on Chinas from this period, other designs consisted of diametrically opposed sets of pinwheels and the early period "solid eye" and "doughnut eye" bullseye patterns. Of particular interest to the marble collector is the fact that nearly five percent of China marbles made during this early period were decorated with flowers. At least six styles of flowers have been identified from this period, and three other styles may date from the early and/or middle periods.

Middle Period (ca. 1870-1890)

As handmade glass marbles became more popular and other types of ceramic marbles such as Benningtons were introduced, toy makers producing hand-painted China marbles were forced to find ways to cut their production costs. Although many of the Chinas dating from this "middle period" were covered with a clear glaze to make the marble more attractive, the real expense was adding the hand-painted decorations. A number of short-cut methods were developed to enhance production and speed up the application of the designs. This included the increased use of the helix and spiral motifs to replace a set of true parallel lines or bullseyes. Both the helix and spiral consisted of just a single line that could be applied as the marble was spun on a tee. Time-consuming designs, such as the pinwheel, had all but died out by the 1870s.

Late or Turn-of-the-Century Period (ca. 1890-1910)

Just about all China marbles made during this period were glazed. Because of the need for faster production, designs became quite sloppy and stylized, and fewer colors were used on individual marbles. The most common design seen on Chinas of this late period were single helixes or "late" bullseyes, and the bullseyes often consisted of just two or three per marble instead of the six per marble seen on the early period Chinas.

"Cheap Chinas"

Another characteristic of the late period was the introduction of imitation China marbles, or "Cheap Chinas." These hand painted marbles were fashioned of a low fired, white earthenware clay rather than the expensive, highly fired, pure kaolin clays used in earlier China marble production. Many of these marbles were glazed, and cannot be distinguished from glazed Chinas. However, the unglazed Cheap Chinas, also known as "pipe clay" marbles, can be distinguished in several ways. Because these marbles were fired at such low temperatures, the clay did not vitrify, and a drop of water placed on the surface of the marble will rapidly soak into its surface, unlike a genuine China marble, which like any porcelain object, will not absorb water, even with an unglazed surface. Another distinguishing characteristic of the unglazed Cheap Chinas is the edges of the hand-painted lines comprising the decorations will be somewhat irregular or ragged, because the porosity of the marble has caused the paint to bleed outward or run.

Group of Handpainted Chinas. $3,500-$6,000.

China with
Handpainted Spiral.
$5-$8.

China with
Handpainted Spirals
with Leaves on One
Side. $10-$15.

China with Spirals,
and Donut Eye
Bullseye Spiral with
Central Band and
Leaves. $15-$25.

China with Spirals,
and Donut Eye
Bullseye Spiral with
Central Band and
Leaves. $15-$25.

China with Spirals,
and Donut Eye
Bullseye Spiral with
Central Band and
Leaves. $15-$25.

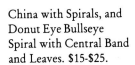

China with Spirals, and
Donut Eye Bullseye
Spiral with Central Band
and Leaves. $15-$25.

China with Central
Single Helix. $5-$8.

China with Central
Single Helix. $5-$8.

China with Intersecting Lines. $10-$15.

China with Intersecting Lines. $10-$15.

China with Intersecting Lines. $10-$15.

China with Leaves (Sometimes Called Birds Feet). $15-$25.

China with Intersecting Lines. $10-$15.

China with Intersecting Lines. $25-$40.

China with Intersecting Lines. $10-$15.

China with Pinwheels. $100-$150. *Collection of Hansel deSousa.*

China with Pinwheels. $40-$65.

China with Pinwheels. $150-$250. *Collection of Elliot Pincus.*

China with Fancy Pinwheels. $150-$250. *Collection of Hansel deSousa.*

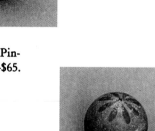

China with Pinwheels. $40-$65.

China with Fancy Pinwheels. $150-$250. *Collection of Hansel deSousa.*

China with Pinwheels. $150-$250. *Collection of Elliot Pincus.*

China Lined, Quadrants with Leaves. $200-$300. *Collection of Hansel deSousa.*

China with Rare Hearts in Pinwheel Form. $200-$300. *Collection of Hansel deSousa.*

China with Rare Leaves in Pinwheel Form. $200-$300. *Collection of Elliot Pincus.*

China with Rare Leaves and Pinwheels. $300-$500. *Collection of Hansel deSousa.*

China with Rare Grapes and Leaves. $300-$500. *Collection of Hansel deSousa.*

China with Bullseye. $50-$75.

China with Bullseye. $50-$75.

China with Bullseye. $50-$75.

China with Bullseye. $50-$75.

China with Bullseye. $50-$75.

China with Bullseye. $50-$75. *Collection of Hansel deSousa.*

China with Bullseye. $50-$75.

China with Bullseye. $50-$75.

China with Bullseye. $75-$125. *Collection of Elliot Pincus.*

Checkerboard
China. $500-$800.

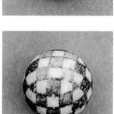

Checkerboard
China. $700-$1,000.

Five Petal Flower China.
$300-$500.

Donut Flower China.
$200-$300.

Six Petal Flower China.
$300-$500. *Collection of
Hansel deSousa.*

Six Petal Flower China.
$400-$600. *Collection of
Elliot Pincus.*

Three Heart Shaped Petal
Flower China. $300-
$500. *Collection of Elliot
Pincus.*

Three Heart Petal
Flower Chinas. $300-
$500. *Collection of Elliot
Pincus.*

Pinwheel and Bullseye Poles Ring
of Roses China. Too Rare to Value.

Pinwheel Scenic China - Farm
Scene. $3,000-$5,000. *Collection of
Hansel deSousa.*

Solitaire Board with Thirty-three Flower
Chinas. Too Rare to Value. *Collection of
Hansel deSousa.*

Pinwheel Stencil China - Priest and
Church. $3,000-$5,000. *Collection
of Hansel deSousa.*

Pinwheel Scenic China - Ship
Scene. $3,000-$5,000. *Collection of
Hansel deSousa.*

Pennsylvania Dutch Style China. Too Rare to Value. *Collection of Jeff Yale.*

Pennsylvania Dutch Style China. Too Rare to Value. *Collection of Jeff Yale.*

Kings Rose China. Too Rare to Value. *Collection of Hansel deSousa.*

Sponge Type China: $200-$300.

Game China. $100-$150. *Collection of Hansel deSousa.*

Bullseye Carpet Bowl. $200-$300.

Scenic China (Probably meant to be a Cane Head). $100-$150. *Courtesy of Block's Box.*

Scenic China (Likely Intended to be a Cane Head). $200-$300.

Bullseye Carpet Bowl. $200-$300. *Courtesy of Block's Box.*

Carpet Bowl with Stars. $200-$300. *Courtesy of Block's Box.*

Carpet Bowl with Crockery Style Design. $400-$600. *Collection of Jeff Yale.*

Carpet Bowl with Crockery Style Design. $400-$600. *Collection of Jeff Yale.*

Lined Carpet Bowl. $200-$300. *Courtesy of Block's Box.*

Lined Carpet Bowl. $200-$300. *Courtesy of Block's Box.*

Lined Carpet Bowl. $150-$250. *Courtesy of Block's Box.*

Lined Carpet Bowl. $200-$300. *Courtesy of Block's Box.*

Lined Carpet Bowl. $150-$250. *Courtesy of Block's Box.*

Section II:

EARLY HANDMADE GLASS MARBLES

by Stanley A. Block

SWIRLS

Handmade glass swirl-type marbles were produced in Germany and Austria in the 1800s and early 1900s, and are the marbles most readily recognized as handmade swirls. These marbles were imported into the United States in huge quantities and were available through mail-order catalogs, department stores, drug stores, hardware stores, and variety stores.

There appears to be an infinite variety of colors and sizes, but a limited number of types of swirls. This chapter will cover the most commonly recognized swirls. Variations, oddities, errors, and uncategorized swirls will be covered later in this chapter.

Little information is available on factories, makers, production facilities, and production quantities of these German and Austrian handmade glass types. As continuing research is conducted, some of this missing information should become available in the future. It is known that glass workers that relocated to the United States produced the same types of marbles for their children after working hours.

It should be noted that any of the following swirl types that are in tinted or colored glass would be rarer than the same marble in clear glass.

The most common swirl marbles are **latticinio swirls.** These appear to have a netting-type core and usually have outer colored bands or strands of colored glass close to the surface. Occasionally, the netting core is incomplete in that it wasn't twisted enough while hot to form the netting effect. These appear as sets of strands or filaments with little twist in the design. The most common core color is white. Next is yellow, then alternating white with yellow filaments. Rarer colors are red, green, or orange.

Open or **divided core swirls** are those with three or more colored bands at the core. The bands can be one color or a multitude of colors. Each band can be repeated or in pairs. The only limitation was the worker's own desire to produce a variety of marbles.

Solid core swirls are those with a solid core of color or multiple strands of color formed into a solid core. If a clear space appears between these bands, it is a divided or open core. Solid cores may also be one solid color or have strands of color applied to the core. At times these colored strands stand away from the solid core, thus form-

ing an inner layer. If the marble also has outer strands or bands, it is called a triple-layer solid core. Three stages can also occur in latticinio and open core swirls, but are more often seen in solid core swirls.

A solid core swirl without any outer bands or strands is called a **"naked"** or **"bare" solid core.** Again, this can also occur with the other types of swirls.

Another variation of the solid core swirl is a **lobed core swirl.** The lobed core is usually three or four lobes, and in most instances, the outer edges of the lobes have a contrasting thread of color such as blue, red, or green. The best way to identify a lobed core marble is to hold the marble so it is viewed from the poles. From this angle, it is easier to see the lobes.

Ribbon core swirls may occur as single or double ribbons. They often occur as flat ribbons without much twist and may also be "bare" ribbons.

Banded or **coreless swirls** are handmade clear or colored glass marbles with bands applied on or near the surface. There may be as few as one, or as many as sixteen strands. "Gooseberry" marbles also fall in this category, with the most common being amber with yellow strands near the surface, usually ten to sixteen fairly evenly placed strands.

Banded opaque swirls or **banded semiopaque swirls** have either a solid or translucent base color with applied bands of one or more colors. Some of the rarer forms have vivid base colors and colorful bands that have made this a desirable addition to any collection.

All of the above marbles occur without added designs. They would be termed handmade glass **clearies, opaques.** and **semiopaques,** and are covered in Chapter 4.

All handmade glass marbles have one or two cutoff points. They occur when the marble is cut from the glass rod it was crafted from, and although it is not accurate terminology, the cutoff points are referred to as "pontil marks."

Lutz swirls come in a variety of types and are a desirable collectible category of swirls. Lutz-type swirls include **banded Lutz, semiopaque banded Lutz, ribbon Lutz, Indian Lutz,** and **End-of-Day Lutz.** Banded and ribbon Lutz are most often clear glass but may be in colored or tinted glass. The opaque and semiopaque come in a multitude of base colors. All of the Lutz categories are desirable but the most difficult to find is the Indian Lutz. This type usually has two or three bands of Lutz edged on both sides by strands of colors. Sometimes these are vibrant iridescent colors.

Indian swirls are normally opaque black or purple glass base colors with applied surface colors. Again, there are a variety of Indians: some with considerable surface color, others with two or three thin bands of color. In addition, if held to a strong light, you can sometimes find translucent glass instead of opaque glass. Translucent colors normally found are amber, amethyst, blue, and green.

There are also slag glass swirls that have a basic opaque glass with applied white threads. This can be classified as a type of Indian swirl.

Clambroth swirls usually have an opaque glass base with applied surface strands of one or more color. However, there are also semiopaque Clambroths that have a translucent base glass. Again, one or more colors of strands are applied. In addition, Clambroth glass is usually an off-white color; however, due to the surface de-sign having uniform strands applied to marbles with black or blue base colors, they have now joined the Clambroth category and are known as black or blue Clams. These usually have only one surface strand color. On a blue base, it is white; on the black base, examples exist of white, yellow, green, or red strands applied to the surface.

Peppermint swirls are marbles that look like peppermint candy and are red, white, and blue with the design around the entire marble and close to the marble's surface. Often, there are two wide blue bands with white and red bands alternating. The number of red and white bands can vary within the marble. Peppermint swirls should not be confused with other types of marbles having the same color combination, particularly ribbon swirls that quite often appear to be ribbon candy in red, white, and blue. Another variation considered a Peppermint swirl is a white base with applied alternating red and blue bands. The rarest of the Peppermint swirls contain mica chips in the blue bands.

There is another category of swirls that has multiple colored strands all around the marble, close to the surface. However, since their appearance resembles End-of-Days, they have been included in Chapter 2.

Group of Swirls. $3,000-$4,500.

White Latticinio Core. $25-$35.
Courtesy of Block's Box.

White Latticinio Core. $25-$35.
Courtesy of Block's Box.

Yellow Latticinio Core (Two
views.) $40-$60.

Yellow Latticinio Core (Two
views.) $40-$60.

White Latticinio Core. $40-$60.

White Latticinio Core -
Translucent Strands. $40-$60.
Collection of Elliot Pincus.

Orange Latticinio Core (Two
views.) $75-$125.

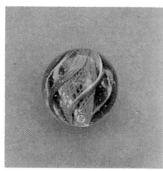

Orange Latticinio Core (Two
views.) $75-$125.

White Latticinio Core. $60-$100.
Collection of Elliot Pincus.

White Latticinio Core. $60-
$100. *Collection of Elliot
Pincus.*

Orange Latticinio Core.
$60-$100.

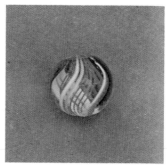

Red Latticinio Core. $75-$125.

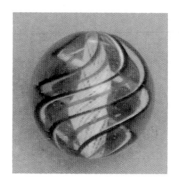

White Latticinio Core - Three
Layer. $60-$100.

White Latticinio Core - Three
Layer. $60-$100. *Collection of
Hansel deSousa.*

Red Latticinio Core. $150-$250.
Courtesy of Block's Box.

Red Latticinio Core. $75-$125.
Collection of Hansel deSousa.

Green Latticinio Core.
$150-$250.

Yellow and White
Latticinio Core. $60-$100.

Orange and White
Latticinio Core. $75-$125.

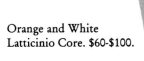

Orange and White
Latticinio Core. $60-$100.

Red and White Latticinio
Core. $100-$150. *Collection
of Elliot Pincus.*

Red and White Latticinio
Core. $100-$150.

Red and White Latticinio
Core. $100-$150. *Courtesy of
Block's Box.*

Red and White Latticinio Core.
(Two views.) $100-$150.

Red and White Latticinio Core.
(Two views.) $100-$150.

White Latticinio with Red
Translucent Core. $100-$150.

Yellow and Orange Latticinio
Core. $100-$150.

Yellow and Orange
Latticinio Core. $100-$150.
*Collection of Hansel
deSousa.*

Red Glass Naked White Latticinio Core. $200-$300. *Collection of Hansel deSousa.*

Green Glass White Latticinio Core. $200-$300. *Collection of Elliot Pincus.*

Blue Glass White Latticinio Core. (Two views. End of Cane.) Too Rare to Value. *Collection of Elliot Pincus.*

Blue Glass White Latticinio Core. (Two views. End of Cane.) Too Rare to Value. *Collection of Elliot Pincus.*

Blue Glass White Latticinio Core. (Two views. End of Cane.) Too Rare to Value. *Collection of Hansel deSousa.*

Blue Glass White Latticinio Core. (Two views.) Too Rare to Value. *Collection of Hansel deSousa.*

Yellow Amber Glass White Latticinio Core. (Two views.) Too Rare to Value.

Divided Core. $60-$100. *Collection of Trudy and Andy Christian.*

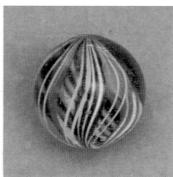

Divided Core. $60-$100.

Yellow Amber Glass White Latticinio Core. (Two views.) Too Rare to Value.

Divided Core. $75-$125.

Divided Core. $75-$125.
Collection of Elliot Pincus.

Divided Core. $60-$100.

Naked Divided Core. $75-$125.

Divided Core. $40-$60.
Collection of Elliot Pincus.

Divided Core. $40-$60.

Divided Core. $40-$60.

Divided Core. $60-$100.

Three Color Solid Core. $75-$125.

Two Color Solid Core. $60-$100.

Two Color Solid Core. $60-$100.
Collection of Hansel deSousa.

Three Layer Multi-Color Solid Core. $100-$150.

Two Color Solid Core. $60-$100.

Two Color Solid Core. $100-$150. *Collection of Elliot Pincus.*

Three Layer Multi-Color Solid Core. $75-$125.

Two Color Solid Core. $60-$100.

Two Color Solid Core End of Rod Tinted Glass. $150-$250.

Multi-Color Solid Core End of Rod Tinted Glass. $150-$250.

Multi-Color Solid Core End of Rod Tinted Glass. $150-$250.

 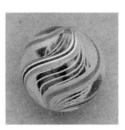

Solid Core Three Layer Translucent Core. (Two views.) $150-$250. *Collection of Anonymous.*

Solid Core Three Layer Translucent Core. (Two views.) $150-$250. *Collection of Anonymous.*

Solid Core Semi Opaque. (English Style.) $75-$125. *Collection of Anonymous.*

Multi-Color Solid Core. $100-$150. *Collection of Anonymous.*

Solid Core Semi Opaque. (English Style.) $75-$125. *Collection of Anonymous.*

Naked Multi-Color Solid Core. $150-$250.

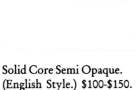

Solid Core Semi Opaque. (English Style.) $100-$150. *Collection of Anonymous.*

Solid Core Semi Opaque. (English Style.) $100-$150. *Collection of Anonymous.*

Naked Multi-Color Solid Core. $150-$250.

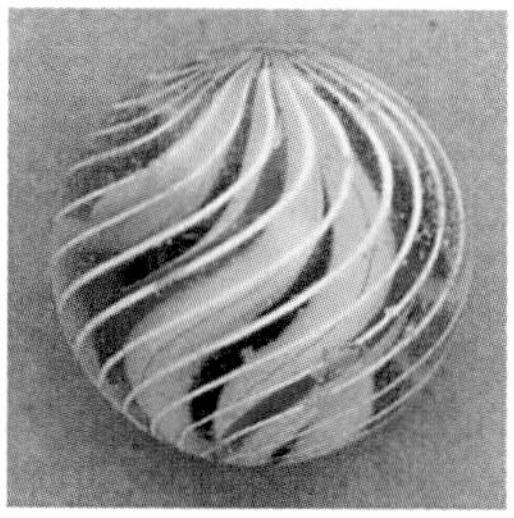

Three Lobe Solid Core. (Two views.) $100-$150.

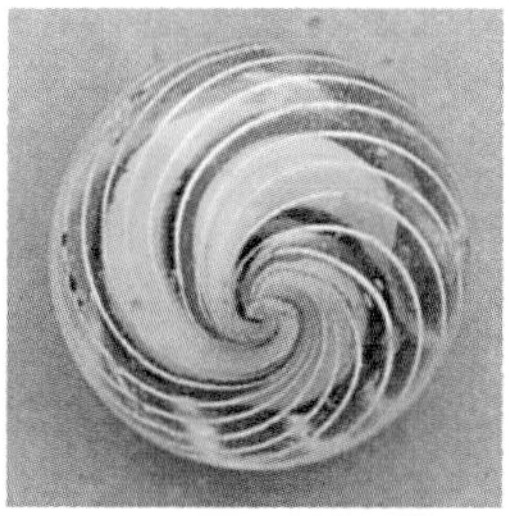

Three Lobe Solid Core. (Two views.) $100-$150.

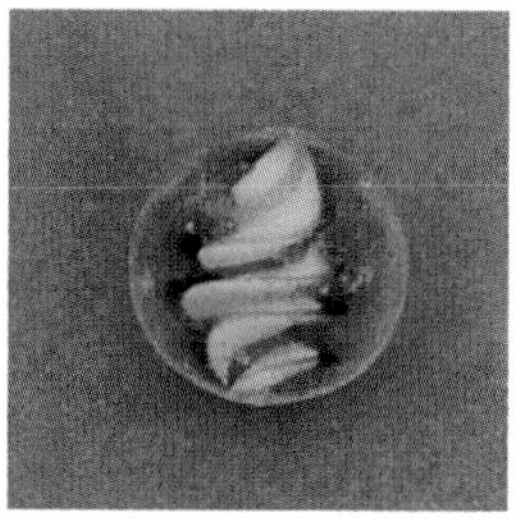

Three Lobe Solid Core with Double Twist. $150-$250. *Collection of Elliot Pincus.*

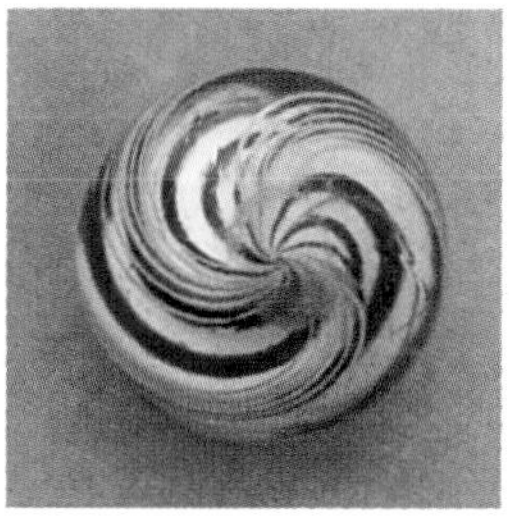

Three Lobe Solid Core. $100-$150. *Collection of Elliot Pincus.*

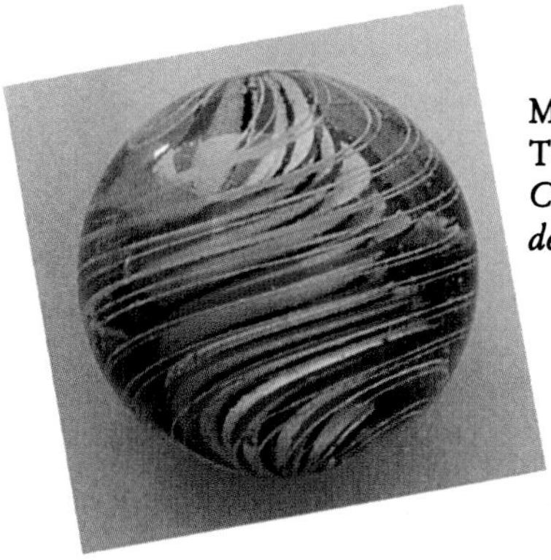

Multi Lobe Solid Core. Too Rare to Value. *Collection of Hansel deSousa.*

Multi Lobe Solid Core. Four Layer. Too Rare to Value. *Collection of Hansel deSousa.*

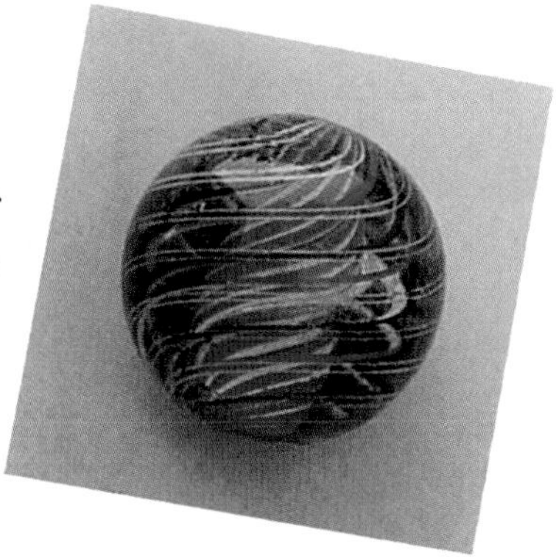

End of Cane Solid Core. $200-$300. *Collection of Hansel deSousa.*

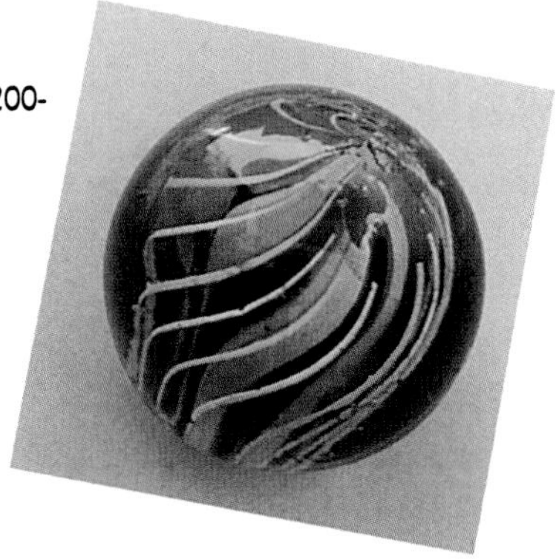

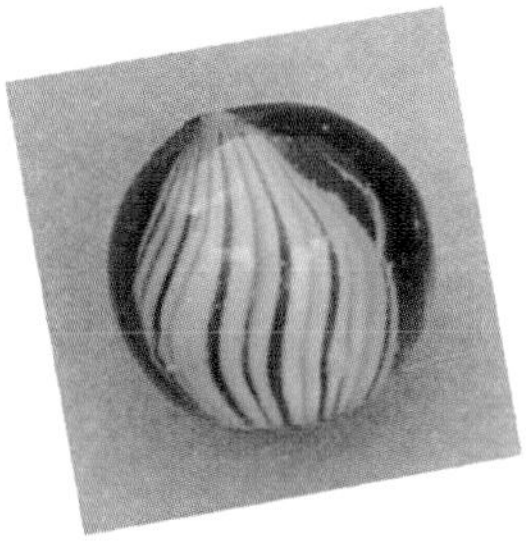

Naked Solid Core in Blue Tinted Glass. $200-$300. *Collection of Elliot Pincus.*

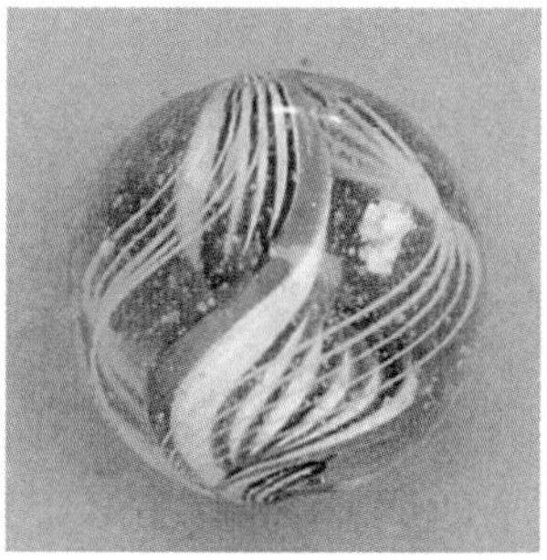

Ribbon Core. $100-$250.

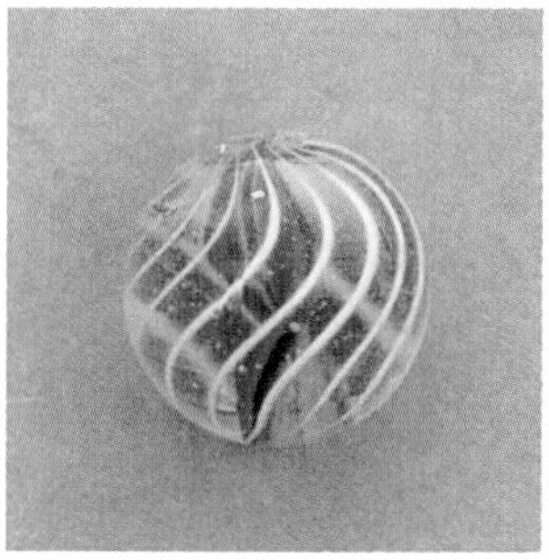

Ribbon Core. $100-$150. *Collection of Elliot Pincus.*

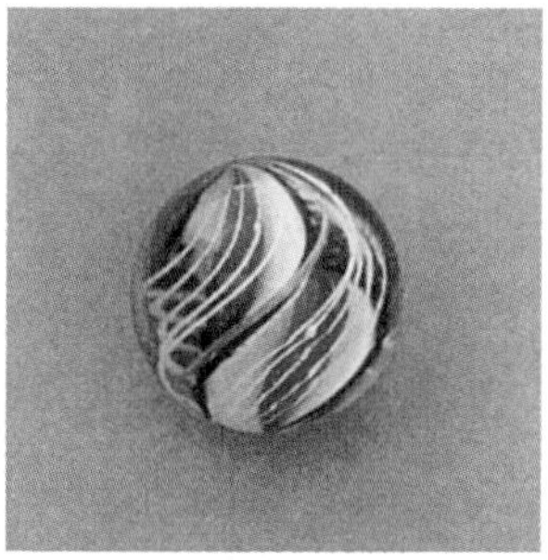

Ribbon Core. $100-$150. *Collection of Elliot Pincus.*

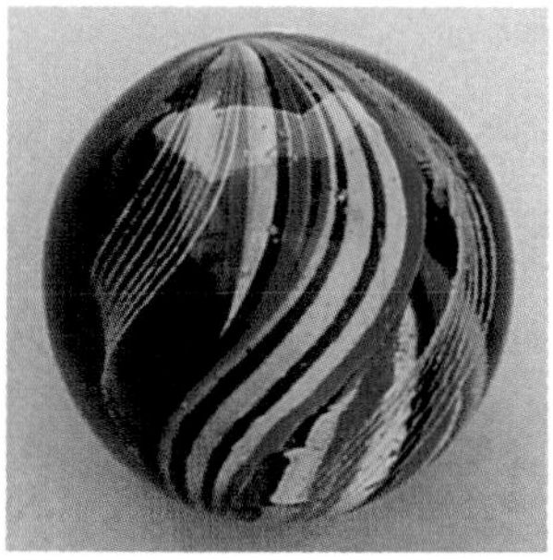

Ribbon Core. $100-$150. *Collection of Hansel deSousa.*

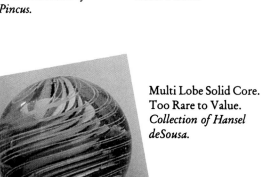

Ribbon Core. Thin Ribbon and Naked. $200-$300. *Collection of Elliot Pincus.*

Ribbon Core. Thin and Naked with Latticinio. $200-$300. *Collection of Elliot Pincus.*

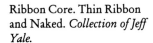

Ribbon Core. Thin Ribbon and Naked. *Collection of Jeff Yale.*

Ribbon Core. Thin and Naked with Double Twist. (Two views.) $200-$400. *Collection of Elliot Pincus.*

Ribbon Core. Thin Ribbon and Naked. $200-$300.

Ribbon Core. Thin and Naked with Double Twist. (Two views.) $200-$400. *Collection of Elliot Pincus.*

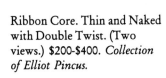

Ribbon Core. Error Twist. $200-$400. *Collection of Elliot Pincus.*

Ribbon Core. Wide Layout. $150-$250. *Collection of Hansel deSousa.*

Ribbon Core. Error Twist. $200-$400. *Collection of Elliot Pincus.*

Ribbon Core. Thin
Naked Little Twist.
$150-$200.

Ribbon Core. Thin
Naked Little Twist.
$200-$300.

Ribbon Core. Thin
Naked Little Twist.
$200-$300.

Ribbon Core. Thin
Naked Little Twist.
$200-$300.

Ribbon Core. Thin with
Two Color Glass. (Two
views.) Too Rare to
Value. *Collection of
Elliot Pincus.*

Ribbon Core. Thin
with Two Color Glass.
(Two views.) *Collection
of Elliot Pincus.*

Naked Double Ribbon Core. $200-
$300. *Collection of Hansel deSousa.*

Naked Double Ribbon Core.
End-of-Day Glass. Too Rare to
Value. *Collection of Hansel
deSousa.*

Double Ribbon
Core. $75-$150.

Naked Double Ribbon Core.
$150-$250. *Collection of
Hansel deSousa.*

Double Ribbon
Core. $75-$150.
*Collection of
Elliot Pincus.*

Naked Double Ribbon
Core. Wide Ribbon. $150-
$250. *Collection of Elliot
Pincus.*

Double Ribbon Core.
$75-$150. *Collection of
Hansel deSousa.*

Naked Double Ribbon
Core. Extra Outer
Bands. $150-$250.

Group of Various Banded Swirls. $3,000-$5,000.

Clear Gooseberry. $75-$150. *Collection of Trudy and Andy Christian.*

Clear Gooseberry with Yellow Bands. $100-$150.

Green Glass Gooseberry. $75-$150. *Collection of Trudy and Andy Christian.*

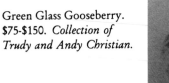

Blue Glass Gooseberry. $200-$300.

Group of Banded Clearies. $700-$1,000.
Collection of Anonymous.

Banded Clearie. $40-$75. *Collection of Anonymous.*

Banded Clearies. $40-$75.

Banded Clearies. $40-$75.

Cornhusk, Honey
Amber Glass.
$100-$150.

Cornhusk, Blue Glass
- Yellow Band.
$300-$500.

Cornhusk, Blue Glass
- White Band.
$150-$250.

Banded Swirl Blue Glass.
$300-$500. *Collection of
Joyce Johnston.*

Banded Swirl - Amber
Glass. $100-$150. *Collection of Anonymous.*

Banded Swirl - Amber
Glass. $100-$150.

Banded Swirl - Amber Glass.
$100-$150. *Courtesy of
Block's Box.*

Banded Swirl - Amber Glass
with Mica. $300-$500.

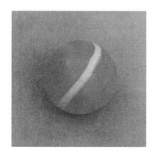

Banded Swirl - Translucent
Blue Glass. $100-$150.

Banded Swirl - Translucent
Red Glass. $200-$400.
Collection of Hansel deSousa.

Banded Swirl - Translucent
White Glass. $75-$125.

Banded Swirl - Translucent
White Glass. $75-$125.

Banded Swirl - Translucent
White Glass Single Punty.
$200-$300.

Banded Swirl - Translucent
White Glass Single Punty.
$200-$300. *Collection of
Hansel deSousa.*

Banded Swirl - Translucent
Custard Glass. $75-$150.

Banded Swirl - Translucent
Custard Glass. $100-$200.
Collection of Elliot Pincus.

Group of Banded Opaques. $7,000-$12,000.

Banded Opaques - White
Base Glass. $300-$500.

Banded Opaques - White Base
Glass. $150-$250. *Collection
of Hansel deSousa.*

Banded Opaques - White
Base Glass. $200-$400.
Courtesy of Block's Box.

Banded Opaques - Orange
Base Glass. $300-$500.
*Collection of Hansel
deSousa.*

Banded Opaques - Yellow
Base Glass. $200-$400.

Banded Opaques - Bluish
White Glass. $150-$250.

Banded Opaques - Green
Base Glass. $200-$400.
*Collection of Hansel
deSousa.*

Banded Opaques - Blue Base
Glass. $300-$500. *Collection of Hansel deSousa.*

Banded Opaques - Blue Base
Glass. $300-$500. *Collection of Hansel deSousa.*

Group of Banded Lutz.
$6,300-$9,500.

Banded Lutz - Blue Glass.
$200-$300. *Collection of Jeff Yale.*

Banded Lutz - Blue Glass.
Thick with Bands. $300-
$500. *Collection of Hansel deSousa.*

Banded Lutz - Clear Glass. $100-$150.

Banded Lutz - Clear Glass. $100-$150.

Banded Lutz - Blue Glass. $200-$300. *Collection of Anonymous.*

Banded Lutz - Amethyst Glass. $200-$300. *Collection of Anonymous.*

Banded Lutz - Green Glass. $300-$500. *Collection of Anonymous.*

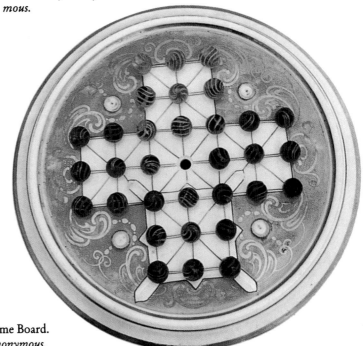

Banded Lutz on a Porcelain Game Board.
$5,000-$9,000. *Collection of Anonymous.*

Group of Opaque and Ribbon Lutz. $16,000-$25,000.

Opaque Banded Lutz - Vaseline Glass. $400-$600.

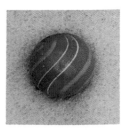

Opaque Banded Lutz - Pink Amethyst Glass. $600-$1,000. *Collection of Anonymous.*

Opaque Banded Lutz - Green Glass. $400-$600.

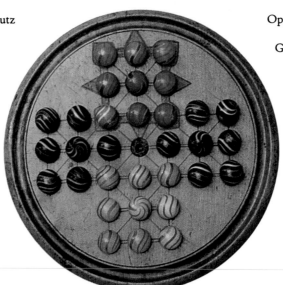

Opaque Banded Lutz - Blue Glass. $400-$700.

Opaque Banded Lutz - Various with General Grant Game Board. $14,000-$23,000.

Opaque Banded Lutz - White Glass. $400-$700.

Opaque Banded Lutz - Green Glass. $400-$700.

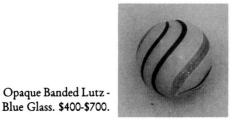

Opaque Banded Lutz - Blue Glass. $400-$700.

Semi-Opaque Banded Lutz - Green Glass. $400-$700.

Ribbon Lutz - Two Color Ribbon. $400-$600.

Ribbon Lutz. (Two views.) $400-$600.

Ribbon Lutz. (Two views.) $400-$600.

Ribbon Lutz - Blue Glass. $400-$600.

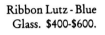

Ribbon Lutz - Two Color Ribbon. $400-$600.

Ribbon Lutz - Yellow Glass. $400-$600.

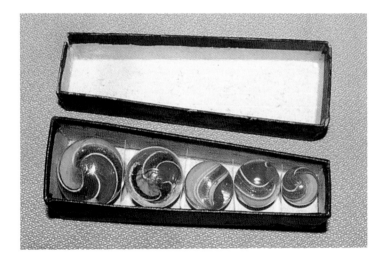

Ribbon Lutz - Coffin Box. Too Rare to Value. *Collection of Gregory Stake.*

Ribbon Lutz - Two Color Ribbon. $400-$600. *Collection of Hansel deSousa.*

Group of End-of-Day Lutz and Indian Lutz. $13,000-$22,000.

End-of-Day Lutz -
Mist type. $500-$800.

Single Pontil End-of-
Day Lutz. (Two views.)
$600-$1,000.

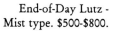

End-of-Day Lutz.
$200-$400.

Single Pontil End-of-
Day Lutz. (Two views.)
$600-$1,000.

End-of-Day Lutz.
$300-$500.

End-of-Day Lutz.
$300-$500.

End-of-Day Lutz.
$300-$500.

End-of-Day Lutz.
$300-$500.

End-of-Day Lutz.
(Mist type.) $400-
$700. *Collection of
Anonymous.*

End-of-Day Lutz.
$400-$700.

End-of-Day Lutz.
$300-$500. *Collec-
tion of Jeff Yale.*

Indian-Type Lutz.
(Two views.)
$500-$800.

End-of-Day Lutz.
$200-$400.

Indian-Type Lutz.
(Two views.)
$500-$800.

Indian-type Lutz.
$500-$800. *Collec-
tion of Elliot Pincus.*

End-of-Day Lutz.
$500-$900. *Collection
of Jeff Yale.*

Error Lutz - Opaque Banded
Lutz. (Missing Normal Design.)
$600-$1,000. *Collection of Elliot
Pincus.*

Group of Indian Swirls. $6,000-$12,000.

Indian Swirl.
$100-$200.

Indian Swirl.
$100-$200.

Indian Swirl.
$100-$200.

Indian Swirl.
$100-$200.

Indian Swirl. $150-$200.

Indian Swirl. (Single Pontil.) $600-$1,000.

Indian Swirl. (360° color.) $300-$500.

Indian Swirl. $300-$500.

Indian Swirl. $200-$400. *Collection of Elliot Pincus.*

Indian Swirl. $200-$400. *Collection of Elliot Pincus.*

Indian Swirl. (80% color.) $200-$400.

Indian Swirl. (360° color.) $300-$500.

Indian Swirl. (360° or 100% color.) $300-$500.

Indian Swirl. (360° color.) $300-$500.

Group of Clambroths. $10,000-$18,000.

Clambroth Error
(One Red Line.)
$200-$400.

Clambroth Error.
(Missing Some Blue
Lines.) $200-$400.

Clambroth. Two
Colors Alternating.
$200-$400.

Clambroth. Two
Colors Alternating.
$200-$400.

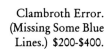

Clambroth.
$125-$250.

Clambroth. Two
Colors Alternating.
$200-$400.

Clambroth. Two
Colors Alternating.
$200-$400.

Clambroth.
$125-$250.

Clambroth. Two
Colors Alternating.
$200-$400.

Clambroth. Two
Colors Alternating.
$300-$500.

Clambroth. Three Colors Alternating. $300-$500.

Clambroth. Cased in Clear Glass. (Two views.) $300-$500.

Clambroth. Three Colors Alternating. $300-$500

Clambroth. Cased in Clear Glass. (Two views.) $300-$500.

Clambroth. Three Colors Alternating. $200-$400.

Clambroth. Four Colors Alternating. $300-$500.

Clambroth - End of Cane. $500-$900.

Clambroth. Black or Translucent Base. $300-$500.

Clambroth. Black or Translucent Base. $500-$900.

Clambroth. Blue Base. $500-$900.

Group of Peppermint Swirls. $7,000-$13,000.

Peppermint Swirl.
$200-$400.

Peppermint Swirl.
$100-$200.

Peppermint Swirl.
$200-$400.

Peppermint Swirl.
$100-$200.

Peppermint Swirl.
$100-$200.

Peppermint Swirl. (Rare
style.) $200-$400.

Peppermint Swirl.
(Beach Ball Style.)
$200-$400.

Peppermint Swirl.
(Beach Ball Style.)
$200-$400.

Peppermint Swirl.
(Beach Ball Style.)
Orange-Red Bands.
$200-$400.

Peppermint Swirl - with
Mica. $500-$900.

Peppermint Swirl - with Mica. $500-$900. *Collection of Anonymous.*

English Style Swirl.
$200-$400.

English Style Swirl.
$200-$400.

English Style Swirl.
$200-$400.

English Style Swirl. $200-
$400. *Collection of Jeff
Yale.*

English Style Swirl.
$200-$400.

English Style Swirl.
$200-$400.

English Style Swirl.
$200-$400.

English Style Swirl. $200-
$400. *Collection of Elliot
Pincus.*

Joseph Coat Swirl. $200-
$400. *Collection of Elliot
Pincus.*

Joseph Coat Swirl.
$300-$500.

Joseph Coat Swirl.
$200-$400.

Joseph Coat Swirl.
$200-$400.

Joseph Coat Swirl.
$200-$400.

Joseph Coat Swirl.
$200-$400.

Joseph Coat Swirl.
$300-$500.

Joseph Coat Swirl.
$300-$500.

END-OF-DAYS

End-of-Day glass usually refers to items that were made with the glass left over at the end of the work day. This terminology has become interchangeable with glass items that have a multitude of colors, or where the colors appear to have been picked up and rolled into the glass in a mottled fashion—in some cases, one color over others.

It is commonly believed that End-of-Day marbles were made the same as swirls—out of rods. Therefore, one marble off each rod had a single pontil. Due to this, we categorize the grouping as **End-of-Day** marbles with single or double cutoff (pontil) marks. The various types under the category are explained as follows.

Onionskin marbles have a base color with streaks of another color or outer colors all over, running from pole to pole, giving the appearance of onionskin ribbing.

Cloud or **Mottled** have overall base colors, which may be one or more, and splotches or bits of colors over the base colors. These marbles may also have clear areas where only the splotches or bits of color are visible.

Panelled may have two, three, or four colored panels. Usually the four panels have at least two opposing panels the same color. They may have one different color in the two other panels.

Lobed core usually have three or four lobes. The best way to identify this type is to hold the marble and view it from the poles or cutoff point, looking for distinct lobes or indentations. They may have up to twenty lobes or ribs.

Swirl-type End-of-Days occur when the color and design are close to the surface and all around the marble.

Single pontil End-of-Days and End-of-Days with chips of mica in them are rarer types, as are some of the swirl types. This is a colorful category that can sometimes be confusing when identifying various marble types.

End-of-Day Lutz are marbles that have the same characteristics as those described above with the addition of gold colored sparkles in some part or throughout the marble. These are a desirable addition to any collection.

Group of End-of-Day Marbles. $5,000-$9,000.

Group of End-of-Day Marbles. $6,000-$11,000.

End-of-Day - Onionskin.
$100-$200.

End-of-Day - Onionskin. $300-
$500. *Collection of Hansel
deSousa.*

End-of-Day - Onionskin.
$100-$200.

End-of-Day - Onion-
skin. $100-$200.

End-of-Day - Onion-skin. $200-$400.

End-of-Day - Onionskin. Submarine Type in Colored Glass. $300-$500. *Courtesy of Block's Box.*

End-of-Day - Onionskin. Submarine Type. $300-$500. *Collection of Jeff Yale.*

End-of-Day - Onionskin - Submarine Type. $200-$400. *Collection of Elliot Pincus.*

End-of-Day - Onion-skin - Submarine Type. (Bottom view.) $200-$400. *Collection of Elliot Pincus.*

End-of-Day - Onionskin. $200-$400. *Collection of Jeff Yale.*

End-of-Day - Onionskin with Floating Mica. $300-$500. *Collection of Carroll Collier.*

End-of-Day - Ribbon. $300-$500. *Collection of Hansel deSousa.*

End-of-Day - Ribbon - Shrunken Core. Single Pontil with Mica. $500-$900.

End-of-Day - Onionskin in Blue (Bristol) Glass with Mica. $500-$900. *Collection of Jeff Yale.*

End-of-Day - Onionskin in Blue (Bristol) Glass with Mica. $500-$900.

End-of-Day - Onion-skin - Four Panel. $100-$200.

End-of-Day - Onionskin - Four Panel with Floating Mica Panels. $500-$900. *Collection of Joyce Johnston.*

End-of-Day - Onionskin - Four Panel. $200-$400. *Collection of Elliot Pincus.*

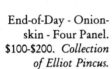

End-of-Day - Onion-skin - Four Panel. $100-$200. *Collection of Elliot Pincus.*

End-of-Day - Onionskin - Four Panel with Mica. $300-$500.

End-of-Day - Onionskin - Four Panel. $100-$200. *Collection of Hansel deSousa.*

End-of-Day - Onionskin - Four Panel with Mica. $300-$500.

End-of-Day - Onionskin - Four Panel. $200-$400.

End-of-Day - Onionskin - Four Panel, Floating Mica Near Surface. $500-$900. *Collection of Hansel deSousa.*

End-of-Day - Onionskin - Four Panel with Mica. $300-$500. *Collection of Elliot Pincus.*

End-of-Day - Onionskin - Six Panel. $200-$400.

End-of-Day - Onionskin - Six Panel with Floating Mica. $500-$900. *Collection of Elliot Pincus.*

End-of-Day - Onionskin - Ribbon. $300-$500. *Collection of Elliot Pincus.*

End-of-Day - Onionskin - Ribbon with Mica. Too Rare to Value.

End-of-Day - Onionskin - Ribbon with Mica. Too Rare to Value.

End-of-Day - Onionskin - Ribbon with Floating Mica. Too Rare to Value.

End-of-Day - Cloud. $300-$500.

End-of-Day - Cloud with Mica. $500-$900.

End-of-Day - Cloud. $300-$500.

End-of-Day - Cloud with Mica. $300-$500. *Collection of Jeff Yale.*

End-of-Day - Paneled Cloud. $200-$400.

Above left: End-of-Day - Lobed Cloud. $400-$700. *Collection of Hansel deSousa.*

Above right: End-of-Day - Lobed Cloud. $500-$900. *Collection of Hansel deSousa.*

Bottom left: End-of-Day - Lobed Cloud with Mica. $600-$1,100. *Collection of Hansel deSousa.*

Bottom right: End-of-Day - Lobed Cloud with Mica. $600-$1,100.

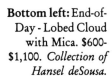

End-of-Day - Single Pontil
Cloud. $300-$500.
*Collection of Hansel
deSousa.*

End-of-Day -
Single Pontil
Cloud. $400-$700.
*Collection of Jeff
Yale.*

End-of-Day - Single Pontil Cloud -
Submarine type. (Side view.)
$600-$1,100. *Collection of
Anonymous.*

End-of-Day - Single
Pontil Cloud. $500-
$900. *Collection of
Hansel deSousa.*

End-of-Day - Single
Pontil Cloud. $500-$900.

End-of-Day - Single Pontil
Cloud. $300-$500. *Collection of Elliot Pincus.*

End-of-Day - Single Pontil
Cloud. $600-$1,100. *Collection of
Emily Mullen.*

End-of-Day - Single Pontil
Cloud. (Top View.) $500-$900.

End-of-Day - Single Pontil
Cloud. (Side View.) $500-$900.

End-of-Day - Single Pontil Cloud -
Submarine Type. $600-$1,100.
Collection of Anonymous.

End-of-Day - Single Pontil
Cloud. $400-$700.

End-of-Day - Single Pontil Ribbon. $600-$1,100. *Collection of Jeff Yale.*

End-of-Day - Single Pontil Ribbon. $400-$700. *Collection of Elliot Pincus.*

End-of-Day - Single Pontil Ribbon with Mica - Submarine Type. $600-$1,100. *Collection of Jeff Yale.*

End-of-Day - Single Pontil Ribbon. (Side View.) $400-$700.

End-of-Day - Single Pontil Ribbon. (Top View.) $400-$700.

End-of-Day - Single Pontil Ribbon. $400-$700. *Collection of Hansel deSousa.*

End-of-Day - Single Pontil Ribbon. End of Cane Error. $600-$1,100. *Collection of Hansel deSousa.*

End-of-Day - Unusual Onionskin with Surface Clouds of Oxblood. $600-$1,100. *Collection of Hansel deSousa.*

End-of-Day. Layered. $400-$700.

End-of-Day - Ribbon Cloud. $500-$900. *Collection of Elliot Pincus.*

End-of-Day. Layered. (Second View.) $400-$700.

End-of-Day - Single Pontil End of Cane Cloud. $500-$900. *Collection of Elliot Pincus.*

SULPHIDES

Sulphide marbles were another type of marble produced during the time swirl marbles were made and imported into the United States. Sulphide refers to the carved or moulded figure in the clear or colored glass marble. In some cases, the figure is also colored. These colored glass and colored figure sulphides are extremely rare. There are hundreds of figures in a multitude of positions found in sulphide marbles. It is believed that sulphide marbles were produced one at a time, and the improper matching of the temperature of the covering glass to the temperature of the sulphide caused many to have heat fractures or broken and missing parts to the figures.

The silvery look to early sulphides is due to a layer of trapped air around the figure. In many cases, this caused larger air bubbles within the sulphide, which detract from its collectibility.

Sets of sulphides in original boxes are rare, as are multiple figures within a single sulphide.

It is recognized that animal and bird figures are the most common; mythical characters and humans less common; and inanimate objects the most difficult to find. However, there are characters within each of the three groups named above that are extremely rare. Those with colored glass or colored figures become extremely important collectibles and in such a case, it is difficult to keep all other factors in perspective.

Following is a list of characters gathered over the years. While it is comprehensive, it is not complete. New figures always appear when we think they have all been identified.

SULPHIDE MARBLE SUBJECTS

Figures may be in a variety of positions, which may not be noted below, i.e. standing, running, sitting, etc.

ONE SUBJECT			
Afghan Hound	Badger	Boy with Hammer	Cherub Head with Wings
Airewolf	Bantam Rooster	Boy with Hat	Chicken
Alligator	Barrister (Lawyer)	Boy with Horn	Child on Sled
Alpaca	Bat	Bride	Child with Ball
Anteater	Bear	Buffalo	Child with Book
Anchor	Bear Holding Pole	Bull	Child with Croquet
Angel	Bear with Ball	Bust of Beethoven	Child with Dog
Angel Playing Flute	Bear with Bat	Bust of Columbus	Chow Dog
Ape	Bear with Fish	Bust of Goliath	Christ on Cross
Ape Man	Bear with Hat	Bust of Horse's Head with	Christopher Columbus
Ape man in Colonial Dress	Beaver	Reins & Flowing Mane	Circus Bear
Armadillo	Bird	Bust of Jenny Lind	Clown
Baboon	Bison	Bust of Woman	Cockatoo
Baby	Boar	Buzzard	Coin
Baby in Basket	Boy	Calf	Coin with numbers
Baby in Cradle	Boy Baseball Player	Camel	Collie
	Boy in Sailor Suit with	Cannon	Colt
	Boat	Caribou	Cow
	Boy on Stump	Cat	Cougar
	Boy Praying	Cellist	Court Jester
	Boy with Accordion	Cheetah	Coyote
	Boy with Dog	Cherub Head	Crane

Crane Eating Fish
Crow
Crucifix
Dachshund
Davy Crockett
Deer
Doe
Dog
Dog with Bird in mouth
Dolly Madison
Donkey
Dove
Dromedary (one-humped camel)
Drum
Drummer Boy
Duck
Duck Flying
Dunce
Dutch Boy
Eagle (thunderbird)
Eagle on Ball
Eagle with Arrow in Claws
Elephant
Elf
Elf with Wings
Egret
Emu
Face of Child on Disc
Falcon
Fish
Flower
Flying Goose
Flying Owl
Fox
Frog
Gargoyle
Gengis Khan Head
Girl
Girl Bathing
Girl Brushing Hair
Girl Praying
Girl Sitting in Swing
Girl Sitting on Wall
Girl with Doll
Girl with Mallet & Ball
Gnome
Goat
Goose
Gorilla
Grouse
Harps Eagle
Hawk

Hedghog
Hen
Hippopotamus
Hog
Honey Bee
Horse
Horse with Saddle
Hunter Carrying a Deer
Hyena
Iguana
Initial
Jackal
Jenny Lind
Kaiser Wilhelm,
Kangaroo
Kate Greenaway
Kitten, face only
Lamb
Leopard
Leprechaun
Lion
Lioness
Little Boy Blue
Little Red Riding Hood
Lizard
Llama
Lobster
Lobster on Rock
Love Birds
Madonna
Madonna Seated on Throne
Mandrill
Man Holding Hat
Man on horse
Man on Potty
Man with Rifle
Marmot
Mary Gregory
Mastiff
Mink
Monkey
Monkey with Banana
Monkey with Hat on Head
Monkey with Wings
Monster
Moses
Mother Goose
Mouse
Mule
Mummy
Newt
Nude Boy

Nude Girl
Numbers 1-9, 0-9
Numbers 10-13
Numbers on Shields or Discs
Otter
Owl
Owl Man, coat with tails
Panda
Papoose
Panther
Partridge Standing
Partridge on Nest
Peacock
Peasant
Pegasus (flying horse)
Pelican
Penguin
Penny
Pheasant
Phoenix bird
Pig
Pigeon
Pocket Watch
Polar Bear
Pomeranian
Pony
Porcupine
Presidents
Prospector
Puma
Punch & Judy
Puss 'n Boots
Quail
Quarter Dollar, 1858
Quasimodo (Hunchback of Notre Dame)
Queen Victoria
Rabbit
Rabbit Reading
Raccoon
Ram
Ram's Head
Rat
Revolutionary War Soldier
Rhinoceros
Robin
Rocking Horse
Roosevelt, Teddy
Rooster
Saint Bernard
Sailing Ship
Santa Claus

Santa on Potty
Scoter (water bird)
Seagull
Seal
Sea Lion
Shark
Sheep
Ship with Masts
Snail
Snake
Sparrow
Sphinx
Squirrel
Stag's Head
Stork
Sturgeon
Swan
Sword
Teddy Bear
Tiger
Tigress
Tin Man
Totem Pole
Train
Troubadour
Turkey
Turtle
Vulture
Washington, George
Washington, George in Uniform, full figure
Weasel
Whale
Whippet (dog)
Wicked Witch
Wolf
Wolf with Shawl
Wolverine
Woman
Woman- Face on a Disc
Woman Sitting on Potty
Woman with Basket
Woman with Basket and Dog
Woodcock

TWO SUBJECTS
Chicken and Sheep
Children Holding Hands
Cow & Calf
Double Eagle
Double Madonna
Doves, pair

Fish, pair
Girl with Lamb
Hen with Rooster on Top
Hunter Carrying Deer
Little Boy Blue with Sheep
Madonna with Girl
    Reading Book
Lovebirds, pair
Peasant Dancers, man and
    woman
Rooster & Dog
Seated Boy & Girl
Sheep with Lamb at Side
Soldier with Musket &
    Spouse

THREE SUBJECTS
Bird, Cat & Fish
Three Bears
Three Fish

DOUBLE SIDED
Bull's Head/ Hunter with
    Gun & Rabbit
Cat, two-faced
Deer Head/ Child with
    Goat or Boy
President/ Running Mate
Squirrel Eating Nut/ Ram
    Lying Down
    when marble turned
    180°

COLORED GLASS
Angel- deep purple
Baby in a Basket- blue
Bear Holding a Tree
    Trunk, amber, blue

Beaver- green
Bird- green
Boar- amber
Buffalo- deep purple
Camel- amber
Cat-cobalt, amber
Cat on Platform- blue
Child- blue, green, amber
Chicken- amber
Clown-cobalt
Coin #2- purple
Court Jester- cobalt
Cow- amber, blue
Crane- blue
Dog- amber, blue,
    amethyst
Eagle- green, teal blue,
    light amber
Elephant- purple, blue
Elf- blue
Fish- amethyst
Frog- amber
Horse on Rock- aqua,
    cobalt, green
Hyena- green
Lamb- green, cobalt
Leprechaun- blue, green
Lion- amber, blue
Lion- brown mane, black
    eyes & green
Lovebirds, pair- aqua
Man Carrying Sack- green
Man Holding Horn-
    amber
Man in Thought on Rock-
    aqua
Mandolin Player- green
#1- green

#2- cobalt
#5, coin type- purple, green
#8, coin type- green, light
    green
#3 & #4- blue
Panther- amber
Pig- amber, green
Pigeon on Stump- blue,
    amethyst
Rabbit- amber
Rooster- blue, amber,
    green, yellow
Sheep- amber, green,
    amethyst, blue
Squirrel- blue, green,
    cobalt, amber
Woman Standing- amber,
    green

COLORED FIGURES
Angel- blue trim on wings
Bear Holding Log
Bird- blue wings, yellow
    beak, on green stump
Boy- red hair
Bust of Jenny Lind- green
    dress
Bust of Jenny Lind- aqua
    dress, red hair, black
    features
Cat- green ground, black
    spots, tail & features
Cow- various colors
Dog with Spots- green
    ground
Dog- green ground, brown
    hat, black spots &
    features

Dog of Flanders- dark
    brown coat, white
    eye, black pupil, green
    ground
Fox- brown stripe head to
    tail
Hen-
Horse- black eyes, green
    ground
Horse- black eyes, red
    mane, green grass
Horse on brown mound-
    black features, blue mane
Jenny Lind- blue dress,
    golden hair
Lamb on green ground-
    black features
Lion- amber mane
Number 1-blue on shaped
    white metal
Numbers- blue (3,4)
Numbers on shield- various
    colors
Parrot- four colors
Peacock- three colors
Pigeon- green pedestal,
    blue wings, black beak
Ram Reclining- green with
    brown horn & features
Rhinoceros
Rooster
Squirrel- brown on green
    grass
Turtle- purple shell
Weasel

Group of Sulphides.
$11,000-$17,000

Group of Sulphides.
$13,000-$25,000

Ram Standing. $150-$300

Sheep Standing. $100-$200

Pig Standing.
$100-$200

Bear Standing.
$150-$300.

Doe Hopping. $400-$700.
Collection of Hansel deSousa.

Bear Begging.
$200-$400.

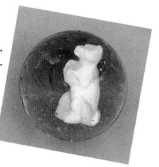

Rearing Horse. $300-$500
Anonymous collection

Rabbit Seated and
Scratching. $200-$400.

Squirrel Eating Nut.
$100-$200

Rabbit Crouching. $100-$200

Squirrel on all Fours.
$100-$200

Deer Biting Back. $200-$400

Rabbit Hopping. $100-$200

Prancing Horse, donut hole type-amber tinted. $1000-$1500

Standing Horse. (Example of Heat Fracture.) $400-$700. *Collection of Hansel deSousa.*

Seated Dog, greyhound type. $100-$200

Standing Dog, sheep dog. $100-$200

Face of a Kitten on Both Sides. $800-$1,500. *Collection of Jeff Yale.*

Panther. $400-$600. *Anonymous collection*

Reclining Male Lion. $200-$400. *Collection of Trudy and Andy Christian.*

Standing Male Lion. (Head Turned.) $200-$400.

Seated Monkey. $150-$250

Egyptian Tomb Lion, standing, holding a pole. $300-$500

Bison (American Buffalo). $600-$900. *Collection of Jeff Yale*

Rams Head. $800-$1,500.

Seated Mouse. $400-$700.

Seated Mouse with Pointed Hat. $400-$700.

Turtle. $400-$700. *Collection of Hansel deSousa.*

Swimming Fish. $300-$500. *Collection of Trudy & Christian*

Flying Goose. $300-$500. *Collection of Jeff Yale*

Lizard on Rock. $400-$700.

Swan. $400-$700. *Collection of Jeff Yale.*

Lobster. $800-$1500

Standing Rooster. $300-$500

Standing Duck. $200-$300

Stork Standing. $300-$500

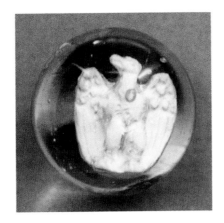

Buzzard. $300-$500

American Eagle with Flag and Arrows. $1,200-$2,000. *Collection of Carroll Collier.*

Gargoyle with Open Wings. $600-$1,100.

Bat in Flight. $600-$1,100. *Collection of Hansel deSousa.*

Baby in a Basket. $400-$700. *Collection of Jeff Yale.*

Baby in a Basket.
$400-$700.

Girl Holding a
Doll. $500-$800

Girl Seated. $500-$800.
Collection of Jeff Yale

Papoose. $400-$700.

Girl Holding a Mallet. $500-$800.
Collection of Jeff Yale

Child on Disc. $1,000-$2,000.
Collection of Hansel deSousa.

Little Boy Blue on Hobby
Horse. $600-$1,100. *Collection of Jeff Yale.*

Girl Crawling. $500-$800

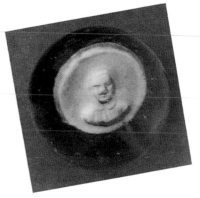

Woman on Disc. $1,000-
$2,000. *Collection of Elliot
Pincus.*

Boy on a Potty. $800-
$1,500. *Collection of
Jeff Yale.*

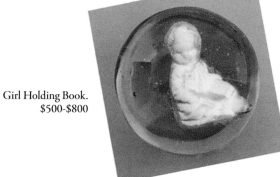

Girl Holding Book.
$500-$800

Woman Holding Basket with Seated Dog. $600-$1,100.

Kate Greenaway. $500-$800

Wicked Witch. $800-$1,500. *Collection of Joyce Johnston.*

Old Woman in Shoe. $800-$1,500. *Collection of Hansel deSousa.*

Santa Claus. $1,000-$2,000.

Seated Boy. $500-$800

Figure on Horse. $1,000-$2,000. *Collection of Hansel deSousa.*

George Washington on Horse. $1,000-$2,000.

Teddy Roosevelt. $1,000-$2,000. *Collection of Bertram Cohen.*

Bust of Chester Arthur, U. S. President 1881-1885. $800-$1500. *Anonymous collection*

Bust of James Garfield, U. S. President 1881. $800-$1500 *Anonymous collection*

Bust of Chopin or Statesman. (Half Figure). $1,000-$2,000.

Circus Clown. $1,000-$2,000.

Standing Man holding Hat. $800-$1500. *Anonymous collection*

The Kaiser. $1,000-$2,000. *Collection of Jeff Yale.*

Christopher Columbus. $1,000-$2,000.

Bust of a Statesman. $1000-$2000. *Anonymous collection*

Court Jester. $1,000-$2,000. *Collection of Jeff Yale.*

Minstral. $1,000-
$2,000. *Collection
of Jeff Yale.*

Angel Praying. $600-$1,100.

Mythical Character.
$600-$1,100. *Collec-
tion of Jeff Yale.*

Mythical Character -
Pan Playing Horn.
$600-$1,100.

Angel Holding Wreath. $600-$1,100.

Mythical Character.
$600-$1,100. *Collection
of Hansel deSousa.*

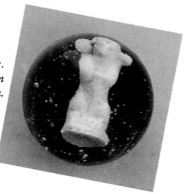

Boy Praying. $600-$1,100.

Mythical Character - Ape
Man in Colonial Dress.
$600-$1,100.

Christ on Cross. (Cruci-
fix.) $800-$1,500.

Number 2 on Disc. $600-$1,100. *Collection of Hansel deSousa.*

Number 7 on Disc. $600-$1,100. *Collection of Hansel deSousa.*

Numbers. $300-$500 each

Pocket Watch. $800-$1,500.

Dancing Peasants. Too Rare to Value.

Pair of Love Birds. $1000-$2000

Pair of Fish. Too Rare to Value.

Sheep with Lamb. $1,000-$2,000.

Three Figures. Too Rare to Value. *Collection of David Terrell.*

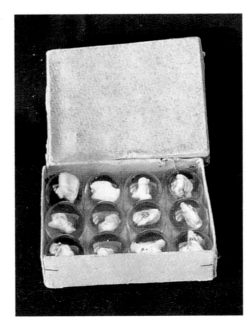

Original Box of Sulphides. $6,000-$12,000. *Collection of Hansel deSousa.*

Colored Figure, Reclining Cow. $2000-$4000. *Collection of Hansel deSousa*

Colored Figure, Standing Ram. $2000-$4000

Colored Figure, Seated Dog. $2000-$4000. *Collection of Hansel deSousa*

Colored Figure, Begging Dog. $2000-$4000. *Collection of Jeff Yale*

Colored Figure, Pigeon on a Perch. $2000-$4000

Colored Figure, Turtle with Purple Back. $1500-$3000

Colored Figure - Pigeon on a Perch. $3,000-$5,000. *Collection of Hansel deSousa.*

Colored Figure - Clown. $3,000-$5,000. *Collection of Jeff Yale.*

Colored Figure - Seated Pigeon. $3,000-$5,000.

Colored Figure - Angel. $4,000-$7,000. *Collection of Hansel deSousa.*

Colored Figure - Angel. $4,000-$7,000.

Colored Figure, No. 2. $2000-$4000. *Anonymous Collection*

Colored Figure - Standing Bear. $4,000-$7,000. *Collection of Jeff Yale.*

Colored Figure, No. 3. $2000-$4000, *Anonymous Collection*

Colored Figure. (Before Restoration.)
$2,000-$4,000.

Colored Figure. (After Restoration.)
$4,000-$7,000.

Colored Glass, Panther.
$2000-$4000

Colored Glass, Rhinoceros.
$2000-$4000. *Collection of Jeff Yale*

Colored Glass, Elephant. $3000-$5000.
Collection of Jeff Yale

Colored Glass, Rooster.
$2000-$4000. *Collection of Jeff Yale*

Colored Glass, Camel.
$2000-$4000

Colored Glass - Seated Lion.
$3,000-$5,000.

Colored Glass - Leprechaun. $4,000-$7,000. *Collection of Elliot Pincus.*

Colored Glass - Prancing Horse. $3,000-$5,000. *Collection of Jeff Yale.*

Rooster on Top of a Hen. Too Rare to Value. *Collection of Phillip, Marian, Scott, and Jennifer Guy.*

Peasant Figure Holding a Long Horn. Too rare to value.
Collection of Gabrielle Paladino

Front   Reverse

Austrian Coin dated 1860. Too rare to value.
Collection of Gabrielle Paladino

Front   Reverse

World Globe with
Sulphide Marble in claw feet

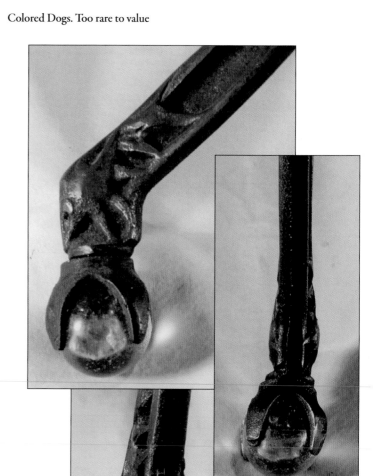

Colored Dogs. Too rare to value

Sulphides in claw feet too rare
to value. *Collection of Gabrielle
Paladino.*

OTHER HANDMADE GLASS TYPES

Blue Mica.
$60-$100.

Amber Mica.
$60-$100.

Blue Mica with
Strands. $200-$400.

Olive Green Mica.
$60-$100.

Mica Mist, with
Strands. $400-$700.

Red Mica.
$400-$700.

In addition to chapters 1, 2, and 3 covering specific types of antique handmade glass varieties, there are also some without any distinctive design, as well as some oddities that will be covered here. **Clearies, Semiopaque,** and **Opaque** handmade marbles come in a variety of colors, or, in the case of Clearies, as clear glass, tinted glass, or colored glass. Since there are a number of these being collected, it can be argued they were deliberately made and are error marbles that had their design omitted for one reason or another. These marbles may have single or double pontils.

Mica marbles were made using clear, tinted, and colored glass. They may have filament or other designs in the core of the marble as well as varying amounts and sizes of mica chips in the marble. The rarest of Mica marbles is the red mica. Next in rarity would be a true amethyst color. Sizes range from peewees (3/8 inch to 1/2 inch in diameter) to 2-1/2 inches in diameter.

Paperweight-type marbles. There are two varieties of Paperweight marbles. The first is a marble having a layer of millifiori canes within it. If the bottom portion of the marble below the layer of canes were to have been ground flat, the marble would be a paperweight. The second type of Paperweight marble is a single pontiled marble with bits of colored glass within it, either in the form of a glob of bits or in an attempt to form a stylized flower as in some early United States paperweight maker's weights.

Error marbles come in all handmade glass types and likely were made deliberately in some cases, but more than likely were the result of the worker attempting to use every part of the rod from which the marbles were formed. When these rods were formed, the design at the ends of the rods either came through the surface of the rod or ended before the end of the rod. Therefore, when the exposed portion became a marble it was not the same as other marbles from the same rod.

Other types of Error marbles were created when a worker was forming the design in the rod itself. Molten glass was difficult to work with and the timing of the cooling of the glass being worked on may have caused portions of designs to be left off. In addition, outer strands of glass, and inner designs ended before the end of the

rod, thereby leaving any number of Error marbles at either end of the rod.

Other rarer type Error marbles occur where two different designs are within the same marble. For example, where a Divided Core and a Latticinio Core are both in the same marble, or two different Divided Cores were used in the same marble. It is believed the worker married the remainder of two different marble rods to form one more marble. While there are not many of these marbles available, occasionally one of these extremely rare marbles surfaces among collectors.

However they occurred, Error marbles are desirable collectibles, and a great many collectors search out these types of marbles. The most sought after marble is the type where interior color design bursts through the outside end of the marble. This type is always a single pontil marble.

Group of Micas. $5,000-$9,000.

Red Mica. $400-$700. *Collection of Elliot Pincus.*

Mica with Translucent Bands. $400-$700. *Collection of Jeff Yale.*

Blue Mica Mist. $200-$400. *Collection of Elliot Pincus.*

Mosaic Marble. Too Rare to Value. *Collection of Bertram Cohen.*

Blue Mica. $60-$100. *Collection of Elliot Pincus.*

Mosaic Marble. Too Rare to Value. *Collection of Bertram Cohen.*

Mosaic Marble. Too Rare to Value. *Collection of Bertram Cohen.*

Banded Mica. $400-$700. *Collection of Elliot Pincus.*

Mosaic Marble. Too Rare to Value. *Collection of Bertram Cohen.*

Mica with Divided Core. $400-$700. *Collection of Elliot Pincus.*

Millefiori Marble. Too Rare to Value. *Collection of Bertram Cohen.*

Mica with Solid Core. $400-$700. *Collection of Jeff Yale.*

Millefiori Marble. Too Rare to Value. *Collection of Bertram Cohen.*

Group of Miscellaneous Handmade Glass. $1,500-$3,000.

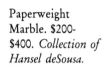

Paperweight Marble. $300-$500. *Courtesy of Block's Box.*

Paperweight Marble. $200-$400. *Collection of Hansel deSousa.*

Paperweight Marble. $200-$400.

Paperweight Marble. (Side View.) $300-$500. *Collection of Elliot Pincus.*

Paperweight Marble. (Top View.) $300-$500. *Collection of Elliot Pincus.*

Clearie. $40-$75.

Clearie. Light Green Tint. $40-$75.

Clearie. Dark Green tint. $40-$75.

Semi Opaque Yellow. $100-$200.

Semi Opaque Rose. $40-$75.

Semi Opaque Blue. $60-$100.

Blue Opaque. $40-$75.

Red Opaque. $60-$100.

Red Opaque. $60-$100.

Rose Opaque. $60-$100.

Turquoise Blue
Opaque. $60-$100.

Green Opaque.
$40-$75.

Yellow Opaque.
$40-$75.

Green Opaque.
$40-$75.

Pink Opaque. $40-$75.

Blue Opaque. $40-$75.

Dark Blue Opaque.
$40-$75.

Lightning Strike. $1,500-
$2,500. *Collection of Hansel
deSousa.*

Lightning Strike. $1,500-
$2,500. *Collection of Hansel
deSousa.*

Section III:

MACHINE MADE MARBLES

by Robert S. Block

MACHINE MADE MARBLES

Glass marble making machinery was invented in the United States in the early 1900s. While mechanized methods existed prior to 1900 for mass producing clay marbles, handmade glass marbles continued to reign as the king of the marble ring. Clay and china marbles were simply not dense enough, nor durable enough, to be of much use to serious marble players.

Prior to the early 1900s, German handmade glass marbles represented the bulk of the marble market. The supremacy of German handmade marbles on the playing field came to an end during the early 1900s as a result of several occurrences. These include the American invention of mechanized marble production, the interruption of German imports to the United States during World War I, and the Fordney-McCumber Act tariffs of the early 1920s.

During the 1910s and early 1920s, marble companies competed to produce the "roundest" marbles: Akro Agate's slogan was, "Shoot as Straight as a Crow Flies." By the mid-to late 1920s, each of the major marble companies was producing perfectly round marbles. Competition shifted to producing unique designs with bright colors. This trend continued for about ten years, resulting in what are today the most sought after marbles: Christensen Agates, Akro Sparklers, Akro Popeyes, Peltier National Line Rainbos. The settling-in of the Great Depression during the 1930s caused marble manufacturers to shift their attention to reducing costs in order to lower their prices and remain in business. The brightly colored marbles of the late 1920s gave way to duller colors, and the industry settled into a maturation phase during the 1930s and most of the 1940s.

Glass machine made marbles were almost exclusively an American product for the first half of the 20th century. It was not until the late 1940s and early 1950s that a flood of cheap foreign machine made marbles, mostly catseyes, began to crowd out American-made marbles. American marble makers were unable to compete with lower cost rivals from the Far East. Akro Agate, the king of American marble making for a quarter of a century, ceased production and closed its doors in 1951. At about the same time, marble playing as a game among children began to decline. Several United States manufacturers were able to survive through this period by producing catseyes

American marble makers were unable to compete with lower cost rivals from the Far East. Akro Agate, the king of American marble making for a quarter of a century, ceased production and closed its doors in 1951. At about the same time, marble playing as a game among children began to decline. Several United States manufacturers were able to survive through this period by producing catseyes and other marbles, however by the 1980s foreign manufacturers were producing well over 90% of the world's marbles. Additional consolidation of United States manufacturers continued throughout the 1980s and 1990s.

This section is presented by company, in roughly chronological order to when each company began to manufacture marbles.

TRANSITIONAL

Transitional marbles are among the earliest American-made marbles. The term "transitional" is commonly used by marble collectors to describe most slag-type marbles that have one pontil. This encompasses marbles that were made entirely by hand, marbles that were gathered by hand but made by a machine, and marbles that were made entirely by machine. Some transitionals were made by gathering a glob of molten glass from a pot onto the end of a punty. The gatherer then either rounded a single marble off the end of the punty, the same as a "single-gather" handmade marble, or allowed the glass to drip off the end of the punty into a machine as another worker cut the stream to create individual globs of glass. It is also likely that some later transitionals were actually made entirely by machine. In this case, the stream of glass came out of a furnace, through a shearing mechanism, and then went into a crude set of rollers that rounded the marbles, but did not rotate them around all axes. As a result, the cut-off mark from the shearing mechanism remained. These marbles are collectively called "transitional." They represent a bridge between handmade marbles and machine made marbles.

Several American companies, most of which were short lived, produced transitional marbles. Among the more well known companies are Navarre Glass Com-more well known companies are Navarre Glass Company and M.F. Christensen & Son Company. It is very difficult to identify individual transitional marbles with specific companies because so few have ever been found in their original packaging.

Transitional marbles are usually identified by the type of pontil. Some of these marbles are also identified by the manufacturer, but this can be a difficult task.

All transitionals are slag-type marbles. They are a colored transparent glass with translucent or opaque white mixed glass. A few of these marbles are a transparent clear glass with colors swirled within. These are commonly called "Leighton" marbles, named after James Leighton, an early marble maker, and are considerably uncommon.

Transitionals are identified by the type of pontil. The seven basic types of pontil, in roughly chronological order, are: Regular, Ground, Melted, Pinpoint, Fold, Pinch, and Crease.

Regular pontil transitionals have a pontil on one end that looks just like the pontil on a handmade marble. This type is fairly uncommon. It is likely that many of these were not made using any type of machine, but rather, were individually hand-gathered on a punty, rounded in a device, and sheared off. If they had gone through a machine, the pontil would be melted into the glass, or likely otherwise smoothed.

Ground pontil transitionals have a pontil on one end of the marble that has been ground and facetted. Many of these are Regular pontil transitionals that the manufacturer took the additional time needed to grind off the pontil. Some varieties of Ground pontil transitionals have oxblood and/or yellow, white, or lavender swirled into the glass, and are referred to as "Leighton" marbles. It is popularly believed that James Leighton developed the colors used in these marbles. The "Leighton" transitionals are very rare. There are currently reproduction oxblood transitionals being produced and finding thier way into the market today.

Melted pontil transitionals are more common than either Regular pontils or Ground pontils. These marbles have a pontil on one end that has been partially melted into the marble. The pontil was either melted manually over a flame or was melted into the marble surface while the marble was being formed in the early marble-making machine. Most Melted pontil transitionals exhibit either a "9 and swirl pattern" or a looping pattern where the white runs in a band or bands from the pole, over the top of the marble, and back to the pole. It is generally believed that the "9" pattern was made by the M.F. Christensen & Son Company and that the looping pattern was made by the Navarre Glass Company. However, since the glass for these marbles was hand-gathered, it may very well be that they were simply made by different gatherers in the same factory. The "9" pattern marbles (marbles where the white glass on the top pole forms a "9") appear to be a little more common than the loop pattern marbles.

Pinpoint pontil marbles are a subset of melted pontil and are very rare. The pontil on these marbles is characterized by a very tiny pontil that looks almost like the head of a pin. The pontil on these marbles was formed because the glass was too cool when it was sheared off and dripped into the rollers. As a result, the cut-off spot did not melt completely into the marble because the marble cooled too quickly as it formed. These pontils are very rare. Occasionally they are found on marbles that are made from two opaque colors of glass, rather than a transparent and an opaque color.

Fold pontil transitionals are also rarer than Melted pontils. The pontil is characterized by a tiny finger of glass that is folded over at the cut-off point and partially melted into the marble surface. This pontil is formed by a process similar to the Pinpoint pontil. The glass was cooler when it was sheared off into the machine. As a result, the cut-off spot did not completely melt into the marble because the marble cooled too quickly as it formed.

Pinch pontil transitionals have a small cut-off line at one pole. The line is usually quite small, about as wide as a Melted pontil.

Crease pontil transitionals are fairly common in relation to other transitionals. It is speculated that they were made in Japan, as some small ones have been found in boxes marked "Made In Japan." Crease pontil transitional marbles are characterized by a spidery crease line that runs along the entire bottom portion of the marble. Again, the mark was formed because the glass was too cool when it was formed as it was dripping into the marble-making machinery. These marbles are likely to be transparent blue, aqua, green, or brown with bright opaque white swirls in the glass and on the marble surface.

For more extensive history and identification of transitional marbles, please see Section Three of this book, and Robert Block's book *Early Machine-made Marbles*.

Transitional, assorted types. $50-$500

Transitional, assorted types. $50-$500

Transitional, assorted types. $50-$750

Transitional, assorted types. $75-$1000. *Collection of Hansel DeSousa*

Transitional, regular
pontil. $75-$250

Transitional, ground
pontil. $50-$300

Transitional, melted
pontil. $30-$300.
Collection of Jeff Yale

Transitional, pinch
pontil. $25-$125

Transitional, crease
pontil. $10-$50

Transitional, pinpoint
pontil. $50-$250

Transitional, fold
pontil. $50-$125

Transitional, Leighton
type. $350-$850

Transitional, Navarre glass type. $50-$250

Transitional,
Leighton type. $250-
$750. *Collection of
Elliott Pincus*

Transitional, M. F.
Christensen & Son
type. $50-$200.
Collection of Jeff Yale

Transitional. Leighton
type. $250-$750.
Collection of Elliott Pincus

Transitional. Fake, reworked
from old glass. $25-$100.
Courtesy of Block's Box

M.F. CHRISTENSEN & SON COMPANY

The M.F. Christensen & Son Company operated in Akron, Ohio, from 1904 until 1917. Martin Christensen was granted a patent for the first mechanized marble-making machine. Many M.F. Christensen marbles are transitionals, because the glass was gathered by a punty and dripped by hand over the rotating machine, which rounded the marble. M.F. Christensen machines did not have automatic feed systems, therefore, the molten glass had to be hand-fed off a punty into the machinery. Later M.F. Christensen marbles do not have pontils. This is most likely due to refinements in the glass temperature and timing, rather than improvements in the machinery. There is no documentation to indicate if the company ever developed automatic feeders or shearing mechanisms.

M. F. Christensen marbles are strictly single-stream marbles. They are either single-color opaque, two-color slag, or swirl. This is because the glass for a particular batch was mixed in one furnace pot, not the separate streams used by later manufacturers. The company appears to have confined itself to marbles of only one or two colors, although three colors can be found in rare cases, probably from when a batch was changed.

The M.F. Christensen & Son Company did produce some **Opaque** marbles. These appear to have been made in limited quantity, and some are transitionals. A close examination of M.F. Christensen Opaque marbles reveals a faint "9" on the top pole. Generally, you can find them in green ("Imperial Jade"), light blue ("Persion Turquoise"), and yellow and it has been reported that there were some lavender opaques produced.

The most common M.F. Christensen & Son Company marbles are **Slags**. These marbles have a swirling pattern of transparent colored base with opaque white swirls. M.F. Christensen & Son Company Slags are easily identified by the "9" pattern on the top pole and the "cut-off line" on the bottom. These patterns are caused by the twisting motion used in hand gathering the glass out of the furnace, and keeping the glass on the end of the punty as a stream of it was allowed to drip into the machine. These marbles are found in blue, green, brown, purple, red, orange, aqua, yellow, and clear. M.F. Christensen slags are found in a wide array of shades of each of the colors mentioned. The brown and purple are

most common, perhaps they were the easiest or cheapest to make. The blue and green are next most common, and are fairly easy to find, while clear and aqua are more difficult. Occasionally, the aqua marbles will have a trace of oxblood in them. Red is more difficult. Yellow is the second hardest to find and "true" orange is the most difficult color to find. Some of these marbles have beautifully defined "9"s. This has been attributed, by some collectors, to the skill of the particular gatherer who made them. There is a wide variation in hues, even within one color, of M.F. Christensen Slags. This variation is much more pronounced than is seen in other manufacturers. It is not known if this was intentional, or the result of the company's inability to accurately replicate color formulas. Some of these marbles are truly beautiful.

M.F. Christensen & Son Company made a type of Slag referred to today as **Oxblood Slag**, although it has been reported that the company named them "moss agate." In reality, the marble appears more like bloodstone than moss agate. The marble is a very dark transparent green base glass with a swirl of oxblood in and on it. Usually, the oxblood forms a "9" and has a tail on the opposite end. These marbles are often overlooked as just dark opaque game marbles because the base glass is so dark and the oxblood does not prominently stand out. However, closer examination will reveal the oxblood. These marbles are fairly rare.

The most popular M.F. Christensen & Son Company marble is the **Brick**. This marble was called the "American Cornelian" by the company. The marble is a combination of oxblood-red and either opaque white, opaque black, both black and white, or transparent green. The common name for the Brick derives because the marble looks like a piece of brick when scuffed up. Each marble is unique in its coloring and pattern. The oxblood-red with black are a little rarer than the oxblood-red with white. There are fewer still that are oxblood-red with dark transparent green. If they are predominately green with some oxblood swirled in, then they are likely oxblood slags. Otherwise, they are referred to by collectors as "green bricks." The most highly sought after examples have very well-defined "9"s and tails. Many examples do not have "9"s at all and some collectors believe these are either later examples or marbles made later by the Akro Agate Company. There are also some very early examples that are transitionals and have a pontil. These are extremely rare.

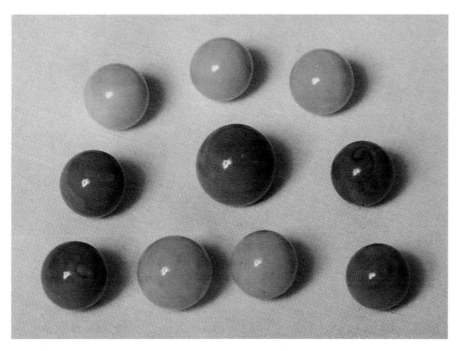

M. F. Christensen & Son Company, opaque. $150-$1000. *Collection of Art Boltz*

M.F. Christensen & Son Company.
Persion Turquoise - Original Box.
$1,250-$2,000.

M. F. Christensen & Son Company, assorted
bricks. $60-$1000.

M. F. Christensen
& Company, black
brick. $60-$125

M. F. Christensen & Son
Company, white brick.
$60-$125

M. F. Christensen & Son Company, green brick. $100-$250

M. F. Christensen & Son Company, oxblood green slag. $125-$350. *Collection of Les Jones*

M. F. Christensen & Son Company, Assorted Horizontal Slags, $200-$2,600

M.F. Christensen & Son Company. Oxblood Blue Slag. $400-$800. *Collection of Hansel deSousa.*

M.F. Christensen & Son Company. Assorted Slags. $2-$25 each.

M.F. Christensen & Son Company. Green Slag Showing "9". $5-$25.

M.F. Christensen & Son Company. Brown Slag Showing "9". $5-$25. *Collection of Hansel deSousa.*

M. F. Christensen & Son Comapany, Original Salesman's Sample Boxes (slags). $500-$1000

M.F. Christensen & Son Company. Green Slag Showing "Cut-Off Line." $5-$25.

CHRISTENSEN AGATE COMPANY

The Christensen Agate Company was founded in 1925 in Payne, Ohio. In 1927, the company moved to Cambridge, Ohio, and was located in a small building near the Cambridge Glass Company. The company had no connection with Martin Christensen or the M.F. Christensen & Son Company. However, the original incorporators may have believed that the use of the Christensen name was good marketing.

Christensen Agate produced a variety of marble styles. These marbles were distributed by the company itself, through the J.E. Albright Company of Ravenna, Ohio, and the M. Gropper & Sons Company of New York City, New York.

The Christensen Agate Company produced only single-stream marbles. All types of single-stream marbles were produced: single-color, slag, and swirl. No evidence exists that indicates Christensen Agate produced marbles in a variegated stream, except for Guineas and Cobras. Many Christensen Agate marbles were made with very brightly colored glass. These are referred to as "electric" colors, and are unique to Christensen Agate marbles. Christensen Agate marbles can exhibit either two seams (on opposite sides of the marble), a single seam (e.g., a diaper fold), or no seam. Little is known about the techniques the company used to produce marbles, therefore it is unclear if different machinery produced each type of marble. No one has been able to identify the machinery used by the company, nor has anyone been able to determine what became of the machinery after the company dissolved.

Many Christensen agate marbles exhibit "gathering" patterns and cut-lines, indicating that the glass was hand-gathered and dripped into the machinery.

Christensen Agate Company produced a single-stream opaque marble they called the "World's Best Moon." This is a translucent white opalescent marble. The marble is similar in appearance to the Akro Agate Moonie. It can be identified as a Christensen Agate marble by two features. The Christensen Agate version tends to be brighter than the Akro Agate version and have a slightly bluish tinge to it, and this version tends to have tiny air bubbles inside it, which the Akro version does not. There is also a Christensen Agate Moon that is light blue.

Christensen Agate produced **Slags** in a variety of colors. These are transparent color base marbles with opaque white swirls in them. The pattern must be a transparent color base with opaque white. If the marble is two opaque colors, then it is considered a swirl. Additionally, the opaque white is randomly swirled through the marble and the surface. If the white is banded or striped on the surface, with little or no color little inside, then it is likely a striped transparent. Generally, the colors of Christensen Agate Slags are much brighter than those produced by other manufacturers. Some Slags have an "electric" color base, usually orange or yellow, which is rarer than the non-"electric" colors. The rarest color is peach, which was not made by any other company.

The most common Christensen Agate Company marbles are **Swirls**. Christensen Agate produced Swirls in a wide variety of patterns and color combinations. The marbles were made by mixing two or more glass colors in a single furnace. Because each color was a different density, they did not melt together, but rather created strata. Since the molten glass was the consistency of molasses, the individual stratum remained as the glass was turned into marbles. There are a seemingly endless variety of colors and patterns in Christensen Agate swirls. Most Swirls are in the 9/16 inch to 3/4 inch range. Pee-wees are slightly rarer and marbles over 3/4 inch are very rare.

White based swirls are the most common, but there are also many examples of swirls with no white in them at all. The marbles can be two-color or multiple colors. There do not seem to be any Swirls with more than five colors in them. Generally, each color is opaque, although there are some marbles that have at least one transparent color. The colors can be dull, or very bright. Bright colors are referred to as "electric." It is generally believed that the bright colors were made earlier in the company's history, while the dull colors were produced later in the company's history.

Occasionally, the swirl patterns form a row, or two opposing rows, that look like flames painted on the sides of hot rods during the 1950s. Marbles with these patterns are called **Flames** by collectors today and are rare.

Another rare type of Swirl is the **Transparent Swirl**. These are a transparent base with another color swirled into the glass. The second color can be opaque, translucent, or transparent. That color is usually electric. Clear is the most common base color, with some red, green, yellow, or blue examples known. The most common swirl colors are yellow and orange, though lavender has also been seen. These marbles are fairly rare.

There are some Swirls that have specialized names. **Bloodies**, which was the name used by the company, are opaque white base with transparent red and translucent brown swirls. **American Agates**, again the name used by the company, are opaque white to opalescent white base with a wirl that range from translucent electric red to transparent electric orange. **Diaper-fold**, a name applied by today's collectors, refers to a Swirl that is a single seam pattern. When viewed from the side, the swirl pattern looks like the diaper on a baby. **Turkey**, another name applied by collectors today, is a swirl pattern that looks like the head of a turkey.

Christensen Agate Company also produced a marble similar to the swirls. These were an opaque base with a series of color bands on the surface of one side of the marble, and little or no color on the opposite side or inside of the marbles. In most cases, the band colors are "electric" and the base can be either opaque or transparent. These are referred to as **Striped Opaques** and **Striped Transparents**.

The "World's Best Guineas" are a transparent F-based (??) marble with colored flecks of glass melted and stretched on the surface. Occasionally, you will see these flecks inside the marble, particularly in seamed examples. It is believed that the name "Guinea" originated because the marble colors looked like the heads of Guinea Cocks that ran around the factory yard. The most common base color is clear, followed by cobalt and amber. Some green-based Guineas have surfaced, but these are very rare, and collectors have told of red-based Guineas that exist, but I have never seen them. The largest Guinea known is 15/16 inch. Cobras (sometimes called Cyclones) look like Guineas with all the stretched flecks of colored glass inside the marble. Rarest of all is a marble referred to as a Guinea/Cobra. This is a transparent, clear base marble with Guinea flecks inside the marble, all on one side of the marble, and none on the outside. Reproduction and fake Guineas have been produced in the past decade.

Christensen Agate Company, original boxes- dyed clays, Albright Brand. $350-750

Christensen Agate Company. Original Boxes - Moons (left), American Agates (right). $2,000-$4,000 each. *Collection of Hansel deSousa.*

Christensen Agate Company. Original Box - Slags, Albright Brand "Professional." (Includes Electrics.) $2,500-$5,000. *Collection of Hansel deSousa.*

Christensen Agate Company. Original Box - Slags. $2,000-$4,000. *Collection of Ron Simplican.*

Christensen Agate Company. Original Box - Slags, Gropper Brand. (Includes Electrics and Peach). $2,500-$5,000. *Collection of Anonymous.*

Christensen Agate Company. Original Box - Slags, Gropper Brand "Favorite." $2,000-$4,000.

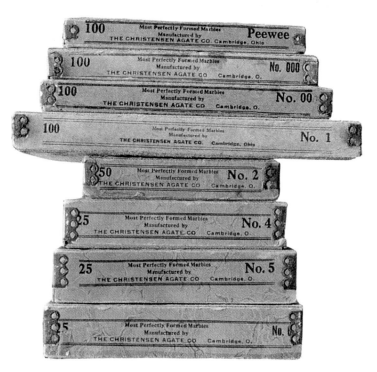

Christensen Agate Company. Slags. (Single Seam.) $20-$40 each.

Christensen Agate Company. Slags. (Double Seam.) $20-$40 each.

Christensen Agate Company. Original Boxes. (One of Each Size). $2,000-$6,000 each. *Collection of Hansel deSousa.*

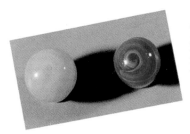

Christensen Agate Company. Slags- Electric Yellow (left), Electric Orange (right). Both Handgathered. $75-150 each

Christensen Agate Company. Slag (light green). $35-$75 each

Christensen Agate Company. Slag (electric yellow). $60-$150

Christensen Agate Company. Slag (peach). $200-$500. *Collection of Les Jones.*

Christensen Agate Company. Slag (red, no seams). $25-$50

Christensen Agate Company. Assorted Striped Opaque and Striped Transparent. $25-$150 each.

Christensen Agate Company. Original Box - Bloodies. $2,000-$4,000. *Collection of Hansel deSousa.*

Christensen Agate Company. Striped Opaque. $25-$750

Christensen Agate Company. Striped Transparent. $50-$750

Christensen Agate Company. Bloodie. $75-$125

Christensen Agate Company. Assorted Swirls. $50-$750

Christensen Agate Company. American Agate. $50-$250

Christensen Agate Company. Swirl. (Two Color, Three Color, Four Color). $200-$1000 each. *Collection of Jim Palko.*

Christensen Agate Company. Original Box with Swirl Flames. $25,000-$50,000. *Collection of Jim Palko.*

Christensen Agate Company. Swirl Flame. $250-$1000. Collection of Les Jones.

Christensen Agate Company. Assorted Guineas, Cobras, and Guinea/Cobras. $300-2500

Christensen Agate Company. Original Boxes - Guineas (left), Cobras (right). $10,000-$25,000 each. *Collection of Hansel deSousa.*

Christensen Agate Company. Guinea. (One Seam.) $300-$600.

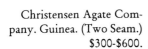

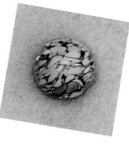

Christensen Agate Company. Guinea. (Two Seam.) $300-$600.

Christensen Agate Company. Original Box - No. 10. ("C" cutout.) $250-$500. *Collection of Hansel deSousa.*

Christensen Agate Company. Guinea. (Single Seam, Open Panel.) $300-$600.

Christensen Agate Company. Guinea. (Swirl.) $400-$750

Christensen Agate Company. Cobra. $400-$800. *Collection of Les Jones.*

Christensen Agate Company. Original Box - Favorites. *Collectiong of Brian Estepp.* $3,000-$6,000 each.

Christensen Agate Company. Assorted Guinea/Cobra Hybrids. $1000-$3000

Christensen Agate Company. Original Box - Favorites, Gropper Brand (front). $1000-$2000

Christensen Agate Company. Original Box. Favorites, Gropper Brand (back). $1000-$2000

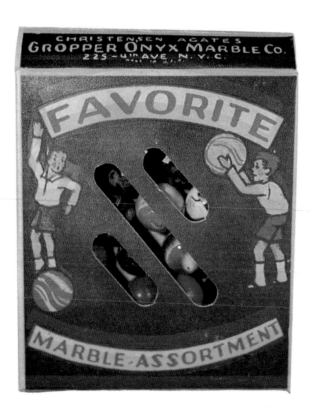

Christensen Agate Company. Original Box - Favorites, Gropper Brand (front). (Oversized Marbles on Cover). $2,000-$4,000. *Courtesy of Block's Box.*

Christensen Agate Company. Original Box - Favorites, Gropper Brand (back). (Surreal Effect of Marbles Pouring from Child's Mouth). $2,000-$4,000. *Courtesy of Block's Box.*

AKRO AGATE COMPANY

The Akro Agate Company was formed in 1910 in Akron, Ohio. It was moved to Clarksburg, West Virginia, in 1914, where it remained until its bankruptcy in 1951. The company originally repackaged marbles bought from the M.F. Christensen & Son Company. By the time the company had moved to Clarksburg, it was operating its own marble making machinery and producing marbles. Following its bankruptcy in 1951, all of the company's assets, including unsold marbles and packaging, were purchased by Clinton F. Israel of Master Glass Company.

Throughout most of the company's history, Akro Agate was the largest manufacturer of marbles in the United States. The company introduced a number of improvements and design changes to its machinery. Some were secret and some were patented. They resulted in several different types of marbles that could not be replicated by competitors. Many Akro Agate marbles are very collectible today.

The company produced both single-stream and variegated stream marbles, in all types except ribboned and veneered.

As with many of the other manufacturers of the time, Akro Agate produced a staggering number of single-color marbles. They produced both clearies, which are transparent clear or transparent colored glass marbles, and opaques, which are opaque colored glass marbles (mostly used for Chinese Checkers and other games). They were produced in such mass quantity that they are abundantly available, even today. In addition, because they were the easiest marble to produce, every marble company produced them, and it is virtually impossible to distinguish between each company's marbles of this type.

The exception to this are a series of opaques that were produced with opalescent glass. Opaque marbles of white opalescent glass were called **Flint Moonies** by the company and are referred to today as Moonies. Opaque marbles of colored opalescent glass are referred to collectively as **Flinties**. Brown is the most common, followed by yellow, green, red, and blue. These marbles are actually semi-opaque and have a distinctive orange-ish glow when held to a light. The Moonies are relatively easy to find, while the Flinties are more difficult. It appears Flinties were not produced in as great quantities as Moonies and these marbles are often mistaken for game marbles by collectors. Moonies were produced by several other companies, including Christensen Agate Company and Champion Agate Company. Flinties can be found in many of Akro Agate No. 150 and No. 200 tins. They were also marketed under the name "Fire Opal."

The other single-stream marble that Akro Agate produced was the **Slag**. Akro Agate produced an incredible number of Slags. It is believed there are more Akro Agate Slags available than those of the three other Slag manufacturers (M.F. Christensen, Christensen Agate, and Peltier) combined. The most common color is amber, followed by purple, blue, green, red, aqua, clear, yellow, and orange.

Akro Agate also made a single-stream opaque-type of Slag called the **Cornelian**. This marble is a combination of opaque red and white glass, and is very similar to a Brick. The color is not as oxblood-red as a Brick though.

Akro Agate produced several different types of variegated-stream Swirls. Some of the Swirls that are collectible today were produced in the same colors as the Corkscrew "Ades" (discussed below). However, the most collectible are the oxbloods. **Oxblood** refers to a specific color that is found on the marble. This is a deep rust red with black filaments in it. The color is very similar to dried blood, hence the name. It is often confused with red colors of other manufacturers. However, those colors are almost always translucent to transparent and do not have black filaments. Oxblood must be opaque and it must have black filaments in it.

Oxbloods are found in Corkscrew, Swirl, or Patch varieties, and are usually referred to by the name of the underlying marble they are found on: Chocolate Oxblood (opaque brown or dark tan base with oxblood), Clear Oxblood (transparent clear base with oxblood), Milky Oxblood (translucent white base with oxblood), Silver Oxblood (translucent silver base with opaque white swirls and oxblood), Limeade Oxblood (limeade corkscrew with oxblood), Egg Yolk Oxblood (milky white base with bright yellow swirl and oxblood), Carnelian Oxblood (Carnelian Agate with oxblood), Blue Oxblood (milky white base with translucent blue swirl and oxblood), Orange Oxblood (milky white base with translucent orange swirls and oxblood), Lemonade Oxblood (milky white base with yellow swirl and oxblood), Oxblood Corkscrew (opaque white base with an oxblood corkscrew, sometimes on a dark blue spiral, which is called a blue-blood), Swirl Oxblood (white base with oxblood swirls), Patch Oxblood (white base with a stripe of oxblood on one side). The Swirl and Patch oxbloods are generally believed to be more recent than the other varieties. Also, some hybrid examples, which are combinations of two of the above, have been found. However, these are extremely rare. Generally, the oxblood floats on the surface of the marble. It is less common to find some of the oxblood inside the marble.

Most other Akro Agate Swirls are virtually indistinguishable from those of other companies and have very little value to today's collectors.

The most common and easily recognizable Akro Agate marble is the **Corkscrew**. This is a variegated-stream marble whose design is unique to Akro Agate. Two or more streams of colored glass were allowed to enter through the marble-making machine's shearing mechanism at the same time. As the different colors were layered coming out of the furnace and because these colors were of different densities, they created separate strata in the glass stream as it entered the shearing mechanism. Just before the shearing mechanism, in the Akro machinery there was a small cup with a bottom hole. The glass stream entered the cup from the top and passed through the hole in the bottom into the shearing mechanism. If the cup was spinning, then a Corkscrew was created, if not, then a Patch was created. The number of different colored spirals in the Corkscrew or Patches was determined by the number of nozzles that had glass flowing through them when the glass stream was created.

Corkscrews are identifiable as having two or more spirals of color that rotate, but do not intersect, around the marble from one pole to the other. A variety of color combinations and designs were marketed by Akro Agate under different names: Prize Name (two opaque colors), Special (three or more opaque colors), Ace (one opaque color and translucent milky white), Spiral (transparent clear base with colored spiral), Onyx (transparent color base with opaque white spiral). In addition, other names have been applied by children and collectors over the years: Snake (a Spiral or Onyx where the opaque or colored glass is on the surface and just below it), Ribbon (a Spiral or Onyx where the opaque or colored glass goes almost to the center of the marble), "Ades" (types of Aces with fluorescent base glass), and Popeye (a specific type of Special commonly found in Popeye marble boxes).

Two-colored white-based Prize Names are the most common Corkscrew type marbles. This is followed by two-colored color-based Prize Names, Onyx, Spirals, three-color Specials, Aces, four-color Specials, and five-color Specials. Although collectors talk of six-color corkscrews, an example where the sixth color was not just a blend of two of the other colors has not been identified. If a true six-color Special exists, then it is extremely rare. Any Corkscrew over 1 inch is extremely rare. The color and design combinations of Corkscrews is almost limitless. A collector can easily amass a collection of several hundred Corkscrews, of which no two would be the exact same color combination or pattern.

Popeye corkscrews are a three-color or four-color Special that contain a unique color spiral. This unique color is transparent clear with filaments of opaque white.

The filaments may completely fill the transparent clear or they can be sparse. The most common colors, in addition to the clear/white, are red and yellow or green and yellow. These are followed, in order of increasing rarity, by red and green, dark blue and yellow, light purple and yellow, dark purple and yellow, powder blue and yellow, red and blue, red and orange, blue and green, black and yellow, green and black, blue and black, or various hybrid colors. **Hybrid Popeyes** are marbles that have three or four colors along with the clear/white. It is popularly believed that these marbles occurred when colors were changed in one of the machine hoppers. However, some of these examples are too perfectly formed to be an accident. They may have been intentionally made by turning on five nozzles, instead of four, to create the glass stream. There are some Popeye corkscrews that have a fourth color, this is really just a blending of the two colored glass streams. These are not recognized to be hybrids. True hybrids are rare and are highly prized by today's collectors.

Some Popeyes were produced when the spinning cup in the machine was not rotating. As a result, these marbles came out as patches. They are the same color combinations as Popeyes, but are actually two or three distinct patches of color on a clear/white base. These are called **Patch Popeyes** and are very rare. These are easily confused with a type of Vitro Agate patch.

There are also several types of Corkscrews that have the same clear/white color combination as Popeyes, but only one other colored spiral (usually translucent red, orange, or brown), and are usually referred to as Ringers or Imperials, and again, are not Popeyes.

The "Ades" are a specialized type of corkscrew. These marbles are a Corkscrew that consists of a fluorescent milky off-white glass with filaments of opaque white and a spiral of translucent color. If the color is yellow then it is referred to as a Lemonade; green, a Limeade; orange, a Orangeade; red, a Cherry-ade; and brown, a Carnelian. The Carnelian is the only one that is actually the name used by Akro Agate. Some of these marbles are really Swirls, and not distinctive Corkscrews.

Another type of machine made marble that has several variations which are uniquely Akro Agate are Patches. A **Patch** is a Corkscrew that was not twisted. It is a variegated stream of glass consisting of two or more colors.

There are several types of Patches that Akro Agate marketed under various names, including **Hero, Unique, Moss Agate, Royal**, and **Helmet**. The Hero and Unique are the oldest type of Akro Agate Patch. These appear to have been produced for a short period of time during the mid-1920s. Both marbles are an opaque white base with a wispy brown patch brushed on about one-third of the marble. The Unique has a small space in the middle of the patch through which the white base shows. The Hero does not have this space. Both of these are readily identifiable by the crimp mark at either pole which indicates that they were produced before the Freese Improvement. These would be dated to the early to mid-1920s. Moss Agates are a two-color Patch. One color is a fluorescent translucent milky brownish/white base. The other color is a translucent colored patch (generally brown, yellow, red, blue or green) which covers one-quarter to almost one-half the marble. An Akro Royal is a two-color Patch. The base color is opaque. The Patch is either opaque or transparent and usually covers about one-quarter of the marble. An Akro Helmet is a three-color Patch. The base glass is a transparent color. The Patch is an opaque color covering about half the marble, and is usually white. There is often a colored stripe brushed on the middle of the Patch. When viewed from the proper angle, the marble looks like a striped football helmet sitting on top of a head, hence the name. No literature indicates Akro actually marketed this marble under the name Helmet Patch.

Another type of marble that is unique to Akro Agate is the **Sparkler**. This is a clear base marble with filaments and strands of various colors running inside the marble from pole to pole. It appears to be made using the same technique as some catseyes, in that various colors of glass are injected into a clear stream as it flows through the furnace. However, Sparklers pre-date all other catseyes by fifteen to twenty years or more, and they seem to pre-date even Peltier Bananas. Sparklers were produced in the mid- to late 1920s and do not appear to have been produced much past 1930. They have generally been found in the 5/8 inch to 3/4 inch size. Sparklers are often confused with clear Master Marble Sunbursts, and can be differentiated by several features. Sparklers tend to have brighter colors than Sunbursts. Also, Sparklers usually have five different colors in them, while Sunbursts have at most three different colors. There is also another marble that is very similar to Sparklers and is usually referred to as a "foreign sparkler." "Foreign sparklers" are discussed in the Foreign Machine made Marbles section.

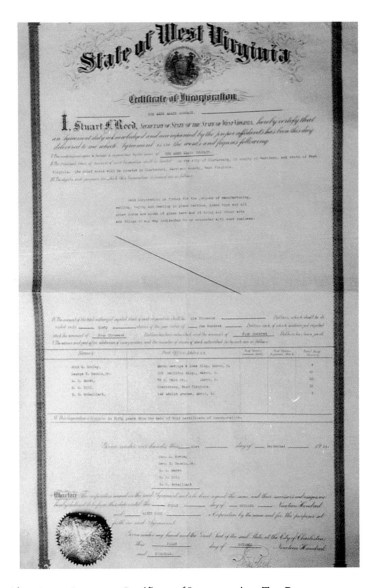

Akro Agate Company. Certificate of Incorporation. Too Rare to Value. *Collection of Darlene & Joseph Bourque.*

Akro Agate Company. Stock Certificate #4 - Horace C. Hill. Too Rare to Value. *Collection of Darlene & Joseph Bourque.*

Akro Agate Company. Original Coffin
Box Containing Opaques. $1,000-$3,000.
Collection of Jim Lyons.

Akro Agate Company. Original Single Box
Containing a Cardinal Red. $500-$1,000.
Collection of Hansel deSousa.

Akro Agate Company. Original Box No. 15,
(Cellophane Window and metal tray.) $1000-$2000.
Collection of Darlene & Joseph Bourque.

Akro Agate Company.
Original box - No. 25,
Slags. (Cellophane
Window and metal
tray.) $2000-$4000.

Akro Agate Company. Original Box - Stock Box, Slags, No. 6.
(Marblized Box, Shaded Logo.) $750-$1,000.

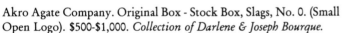

Akro Agate Company. Original Box - Stock Box,
Slags, No. 2. (Marblized Box, Shaded Logo, Edge Flap
is Mis-spelled "Assorted Oynx.") $600-$1,200.

Akro Agate Company. Original Box - Stock Box, Slags, No. 0. (Small
Open Logo). $500-$1,000. *Collection of Darlene & Joseph Bourque.*

Akro Agate Company. Original Box - Jobber Box. (M. Gropper
& Son), "Cerise Agates." (Contains Cornelians.) $500-$1000

Akro Agate Company. Original Box- Presentation Box.
(Cardinal Red.) $350-$1250

Akro Agate Company. Patch - Unique (left), Hero (right). $75-$100 each. *Collection of Darlene & Joseph Bourque.*

Akro Agate Company. Patch - The "Birds" of Akro Agate. (Uniques and Heroes.) $100-$200 each. *Collection of Darlene & Joseph Bourque.*

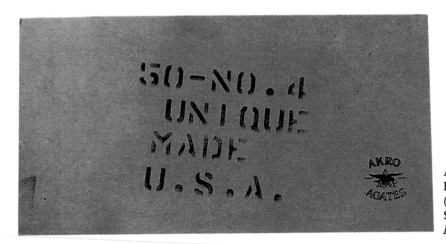

Akro Agate Company. Original Box - Stock Box, Unique. (Stenciled, Small Open Logo.) $1,500-$3,000. *Collection of Darlene & Joseph Bourque.*

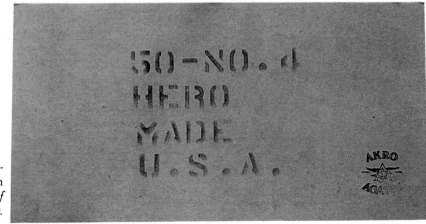

Akro Agate Company. Original Box - Stock Box, Hero (Stenciled, Small Open Logo.) $1,500-$3,000. *Collection of Darlene & Joseph Bourque.*

Akro Agate Company. Original Box - Stock Box, Unique. (Grebe.) $1,500-$3,000. *Collection of Darlene & Joseph Bourque.*

Akro Agate Company. Original Box - Stock Box, Hero. (Brown Thrasher.) $1,500-$3,000. *Collection of Darlene & Joseph Bourque.*

Akro Agate Company. Original Box - Stock Box, Hero. (Golden Tawny.) $1,000-$3,000. *Collection of Darlene & Joseph Bourque.*

Akro Agate Company. Original Box - Stock Box, Hero. (Rainbow.) $1,500-$3,000. *Collection of Darlene & Joseph Bourque.*

Akro Agate Company.
Patch - Experimental.
$75-$150

Akro Agate Company.
Patch - Experimental.
$100-$250

Akro Agate Company.
Patch -Experimental.
$100-$250

Akro Agate Company.
Patch - Experimental.
$125-$300. *Courtesy of
Block's Box.*

Akro Agate Company.
Patch - Moss Agate.
$5-$50

Akro Agate Company. Original Box - Stock Box, Moss Agates, No.1. (Open Multicolor Logo,
Fancy Box.) $650-$1250. *Collection of Darlene & Joseph Bourque.*

Akro Agate Company. Original
Box - Stock Box, Royals, No. 2.
(No Logo.) $750-$1,500.
Collection of Hansel deSousa.

Akro Agate Company. Original
Box - Stock Box, Royals, No. 1.
(Marblized Box, Shaded Logo.)
$750-$1,500. *Collection of Darlene
& Joseph Bourque.*

Akro Agate Company. Original
Box - Stock Box, Unique, No. 4.
(Open Logo.) $600-$1,200.
Courtesy of Block's Box.

Akro Agate Company.
Patch - Helmet. $2-$25.

Akro Agate Company. Original Box - Stock Box, Tri-color patch, No. 0.
(Open Logo.) $400-$800. *Collection of Darlene & Joseph Bourque.*

Akro Agate Company.
Patch - Popeye. $150-$300.

Akro Agate Company. Corkscrew - Two color.
(White Base.) $2-$25

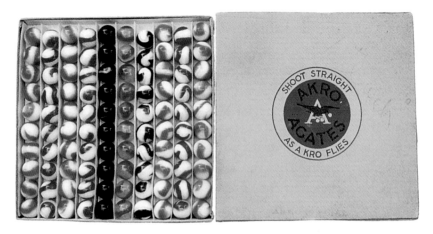

Akro Agate Company. Corkscrew - Two Color. (Black Spiral.) $15-$50. *Collection of Cathy Runyan Svacina.*

Akro Agate Company. Original Box - Stock Box, Corkscrews, No. 1. (Open Multi-Color Logo.) $600-$1,200. *Collection of Darlene & Joseph Bourque.*

Akro Agate Company. Corkscrew - Three color. $15-$75

Akro Agate Company. Corkscrew - Two Color. (Color Base.) $5-$50

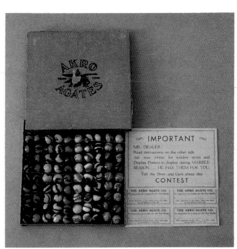

Akro Agate Company. Original Box - Stock Box, Corkscrews, No. 1. (Shaded Logo, Contest Insert.) $750-$1500. *Courtesy of Block'x Box.*

Akro Agate Company. Original Box - Stock Box, Corkscrews, No. 1. (Marblized Box, Shaded Logo.) $800-$1750. *Collection of David Freburg.*

Akro Agate Company. Corkscrew - Snakes.
$10-$50 each.

Akro Agate Company. Corkscrew - Aces.
$40-$150 each.

Akro Agate Company. Corkscrew - Ribbons.
(Clear Base.) $10-$75

Akro Agate Company. Corkscrew -Ades.
$10-$125

Akro Agate Company. Corkscrew - Ribbons.
$10-$75 each.

Akro Agate Company. Corkscrew - Assortment of Limeade,
Cherryade, and Tri-color Ace shooters. $75-$250 each.

Akro Agate Company. Corkscrew - Popeyes. $15-$250 each.

Akro Agate Company. Corkscrew - Two Color. (Moonie Base.) $50-$175.

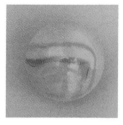

Akro Agate Company. Corkscrew - Two Color. (Early Colors.) $45-$150.

Akro Agate Company. Corkscrew-Two Color. (Early Colors.) $45-$150.

Akro Agate Company. Corkscrew - Popeyes. (Hybrids.) $80-$500 each.

Akro Agate Company. Corkscrew - Ringer (top), Imperial (bottom left and right). $10-$60.

Akro Agate Company. Corkscrew - Experimental. $150-$300

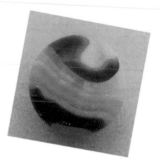

Akro Agate Company. Corkscrew - Lemonade/ Cherryade hybrid. $100-$250. Courtesy of Block's Box.

Akro Agate Company. Swirl - Tri-color. $25-$125. Courtesy Block's Box.

Akro Agate Company. Swirl - Llimeade. $20-$100. *Courtesy of Block's box.*

Akro Agate Company. Cornelian. Red (left), orange (right). $50-$200. Courtesy of Chip Off the Old Block.

Akro Agate Company. Original Box - Presentation Box. Carnelian. (Fancy Embossed Logo.) $1,000-$2,000.

Akro Agate Company. Original Box - Presentation Box, Cornelian. (Shaded Logo.) $1,500-$3,000. *Collection of Hansel deSousa.*

Akro Agate Company. Original Box - Presentation Box, Carnelian, Plain Texture Cover (top), Leatherized Cover (bottom). (Open Logo.) $1,000-$2,000. *Collection of Hansel deSousa.*

Akro Agate Company. Carnelian. $20-$150.

Akro Agate Company. Oxblood - Milky. (Double Ingot Error.) $30-$60.

Akro Agate Company. Assorted Oxbloods. $15-$500 each.

Akro Agate Company. Assorted Flinties. $10-$75. *Courtesy of Block's Box.*

Akro Agate Company. Oxblood - Egg Yolk. $100-$250.

Akro Agate Company. Original Box - Jobber "Sample Kit." (M. Gropper & Son, Closed). Too Rare to Value. *Collection of Hansel deSousa.*

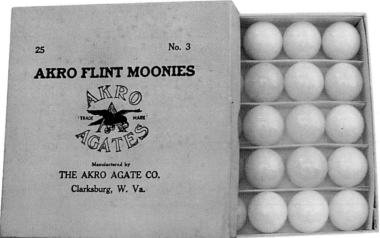

Akro Agate Company. Original Box - Presentation Box, Flint Moonies. (Shaded Logo.) $1500-$3000. *Collection of Darlene & Joseph Bourque.*

Akro Agate Company. Moonie. $5-$25.

Akro Agate Company. Original Box - Jobber "Sample Kit." (M. Gropper & Son, Open). Too Rare to Value. *Collection of Hansel deSousa.*

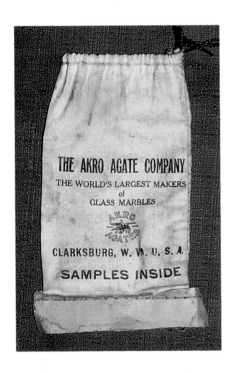

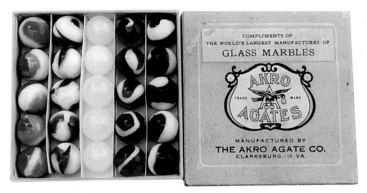

Akro Agate Company. Original Box - Sampler. $3,500-
$7,000. *Collection of Darlene & Joseph Bourque.*

Akro Agate Company. Original Bag
- Sampler. Too Rare to Value.
Collection of David Freburg.

Akro Agate Company. Original Box - Gift Set. (Cellophane
window.) $12,500-$25,000. *Collection of Darlene & Joseph
Bourque.*

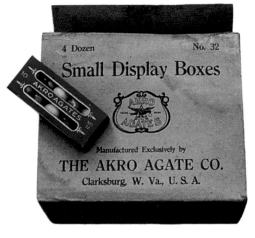

Akro Agate Company. Original Boxes - Sleeves, No. 16. Advertising, No. 16,
No. A-16, No. 20, No. 32, No. 64. $100-$500 each.

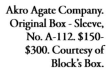

Akro Agate Company.
Original Box - Sleeve,
No. A-112. $150-
$300. Courtesy of
Block's Box.

Akro Agate Company. Original Box - Shipping
Case, No. 32 Sleeves. $5,000-$10,000. *Collection
of Darlene & Joseph Bourque.*

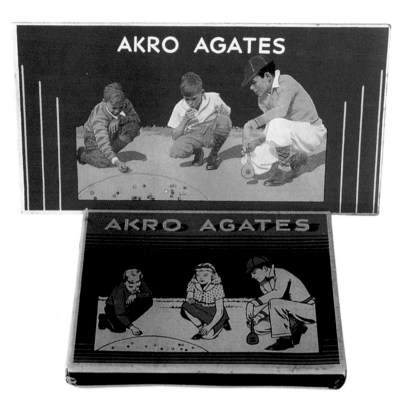

Akro Agate Company. Original Box. No.230 (bottom). No. 300 (top). (Both Early.) $1000-$4000 each. Collection of Hansel deSousa.

Akro Agate Company. Original Box - No. 230. (Cellophane window.) $1,500-$3,000. *Collection of Darlene & Joseph Bourque.*

Akro Agate Company. Original Box - Gift Box, No. 250. (Early.) $1,000-$2,000. *Collection of Darlene & Joseph Bourque.*

Akro Agate Company. Original Box - Gift Box, No. 230. (Early.) $1,000-$2,000.

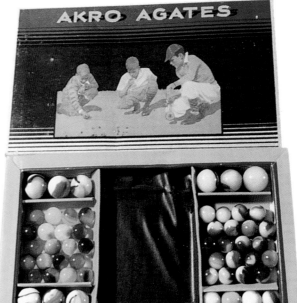

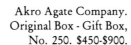

Akro Agate Company.
Original Box - Gift Box,
No. 250. $450-$900.

Akro Agate Company. Original Box -
Gift Box, No. 230. $350-$700.

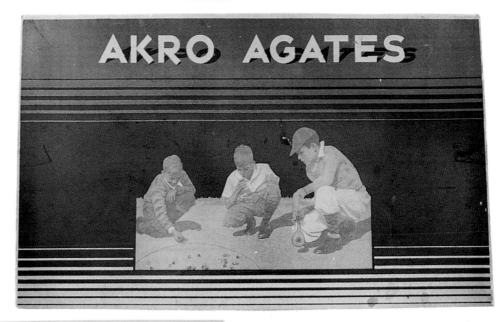

Akro Agate Company. Original Box - Gift
Box, No. 300. (Box Top.) *Collection of
Darlene & Joseph Bourque.*

Akro Agate Company. Original Box - Gift
Box, No.300. (Box Bottom.) $800-$2000.

Akro Agate Company. Original Box - Gift Tin, No. 150.
(Tin Top.) $300-$900.

Akro Agate
Company.
Original Box -
Gift Box, Black
and Silver. $500-
$2,000.

Akro Agate Company. Original Box - Gift Tin, No. 200.
(Inside.) $450-$1,200. *Collection of Darlene & Joseph
Bourque.*

Akro Agate Company. Original Box - Gift Box, No. 125.
(With Bag.) $500-$1000. Collection of Hansel deSousa.

Akro Agate Company.
Original Box - Gift Box,
No. 125. (Without Bag).
$450-$900.

Akro Agate Company. Original Box - Gift Tin, No. 200. (Inside.) $1000-$2000.

Akro Agate Company. Original Box - Popeye. (Yellow.) $750-$2000.

Akro Agate Company. Original Box - Popeye. (Prototype.) $6,000-$12,000.

Akro Agate Company. Original Box - Ringer. $1,000-$2,000. *Collection of Anonymous.*

Akro Agate Company. Original Box - Gift Box. (Stained Glass Design.) $3,500-$7,000. *Collection of Brian Merhar.*

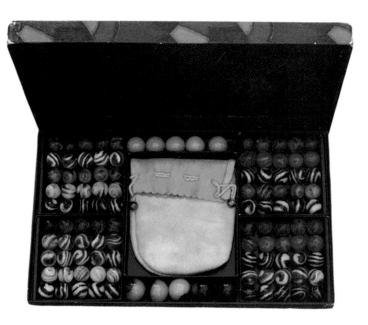

Top left: Akro Agate Company. Original Box - Gift Box. (Box Top, Stained Glass Design.) $1,500-$3,000. *Collection of Hansel deSousa.*

Top right: Akro Agate Company. Original Box - Gift Box. (Inside, Stained Glass Design.) $1,500-3,000. *Collection of Hansel deSousa.*

Center left: Akro Agate Company. Original Box - Gift Box. (Stained Glass Design.) $1,500-$3,000. *Collection of Ron Simplican.*

Center right: Akro Agate Company. Original Box - Gift Box. (Stained Glass Design.) $1,000-$3,000. *Collection of Hansel deSousa.*

Bottom right: Akro Agate Company. Original Box - Gift Box. (Stained Glass Design.) $1,500-$3,000. *Collection of Hansel deSousa.*

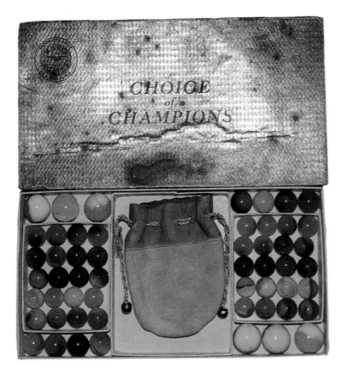

Akro Agate Company. Original Box - Chinese Checkers. (Tan, Red. White.) $20-$100 each.

Akro Agate Company. Original Box - Gift Box. Silver. $1,500-$3,000. *Collection of David Freburg.*

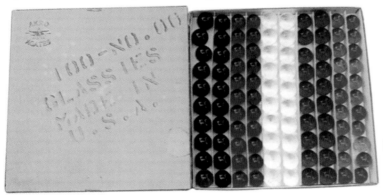

Akro Agate Company. Original Box - Stock Box, Glassies. (Small Open Stenciled Logo.) $350-$700. *Collection of Darlene & Joseph Bourque.*

Akro Agate Company. Original Bag - Hot Shot (Patch), Mesh. $100-$200. *Courtesy of Chip Off the Old Block.*

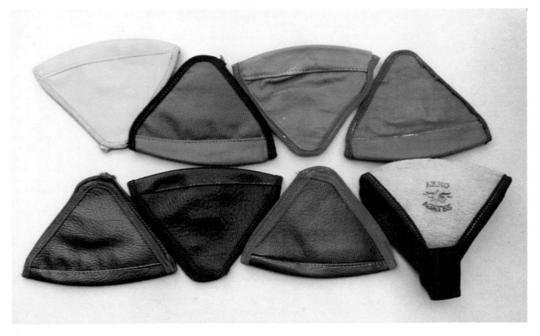

Akro Agate Company. Kneepads. $100-$300 each. *Collection of Darlene & Joseph Bourque.*

Akro Agate Company. Original Box - Store Sales Display. (Bubble Gum Box.) $3,500-$7,000. *Collection of Darlene & Joseph Bourque.*

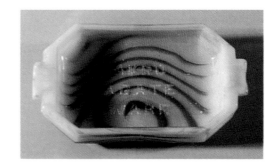

Akro Agate Company. Akroware. $225-$450.

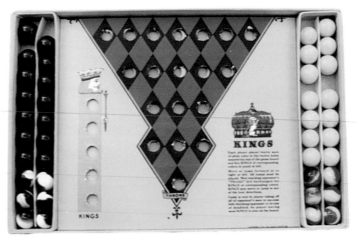

Akro Agate Company. Akroware. $150-$300.

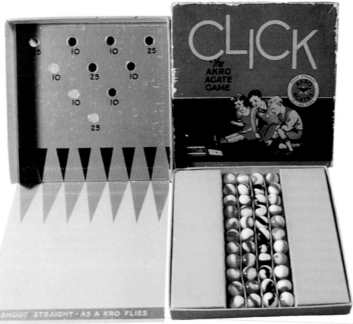

Akro Agate Company. Original Game - Click. $150-$300.

Akro Agate Company. Original Game -Kings. (Inside.) $400-$800. Collection of Darlene & Joseph Bourque.

Akro Agate Company. Original Game - Kings. $400-$800.

PELTIER GLASS COMPANY

The Peltier Glass Company was founded in 1886 under the name The Novelty Glass Company by Victor Peltier. The name was changed to the Peltier Glass Company in 1919. The company is located in Ottawa, Illinois, and is still in operation, but no longer produces playing marbles.

Peltier began making marbles sometime during the early 1920s. Their marbles were marketed under the Peltier name and also by M. Gropper & Sons. Peltier produced Slags, Patches, Ribbons, and Catseyes. Peltier also produced Clearies and Opaques, but there is no recognized way to identify them as specific to this company.

The earliest Peltier marbles are single-stream. Peltier produced single-stream Slags and Swirls.

Peltier **Slags** are single-stream marbles, as are the Slags of other companies. They are transparent colored based glass with opaque white swirled in. Peltier Slags are rarer than those of other companies. The most common are brown, blue, or green. They can also be found in aqua, purple, red, and yellow. The company does not appear to have produced clear Slags. Peltier Slags are readily identifiable by the very fine feathering pattern produced by the white swirls. This is unique to Peltier. Their Slags, as with many Peltier marbles, also tend to have blown out air holes which are much less common in the marbles of other companies.

Peltier produced several types of single-stream Swirls. These are referred to as **"Miller machine"** marbles because they were produced on Peltier's first marble machine designed by William Miller. Peltier used other types of machines to produce Rainbos, etc. Those machines do not have a name.

An early type of Peltier multi-color swirl was produced by the "Miller machine." It has a transparent color base with several opaque colors swirled in, it is much rarer than more common multi-colors where the colors are actually ribbons, not swirls. There are several types of multi-color Swirls that have similar coloring to tri-color and two-color National Line Rainbos. These are also rare. Another type of "Miller machine" Swirl is called a Honey Onyx. These are semi-opaque white base with a thin translucent brown patch and a thin translucent green stripe on the marble. They are rare as well.

Peltier produced a Patch marble which they marketed as the **Peerless**, and which are very collectible today. The marbles are a two-color Patch. They are identifiable by the uniqueness of their shades of color and by their design. Peerless Patches are the type of marble that Peltier Picture Marbles (comics) are on. The most common color combinations are black patch on white, green patch on

mustard yellow, transparent green patch on white, red on white, yellow on aqua, or red on aqua. There are other color combinations, but they are rarer. The rarest patch color is called "pearlized." This is a greenish color that has a satin shimmer or sheen to it. These are very rare. The design of the patch on Peerless Patches is unique. The patches of other companies have straight edges. Peltier marbles have patches that have curved or "S" edges. This feature, along with the unique colors, makes Peerless Patches easily identifiable.

One of the most collectible Peltier Glass marbles is the **Picture Marble** or comic. These are Peltier Peerless Patches with a black transfer of one of twelve different King Syndicate comic characters fired on the marble surface. Usually, there is an overglaze of clear glass. The twelve characters (in ascending order of rarity) are Emma, Koko, Bimbo, Andy, Smitty, Annie, Herbie, Sandy, Skeezix, Betty, Moon, Kayo. There are also comic marbles with a transfer of Tom Mix and with an advertisement for Cotes Master Loaf on them. These two are very rare. The transfers are always on 19/32 inch to 11/16 inch Peerless Patches. Each character has a specific marble color combination that is most common to that marble. Rarer color combinations are difficult to find. Also, there has been a Tom Mix marble reported to have a red transfer, a black comic transfer on a 7/8 inch marble. These are extremely rare, and were probably experimental.

The majority of collectible Peltier Glass Company marbles are ribboned type. The most collectible of these are the **National Line Rainbo**. These marbles are an opaque base color with four to six thin ribbons in the surface. The tri-colors can be distinguished from "Miller Machine" marbles because they have two seams on them, as if they were two halves that were joined together. Also, the ribbons are usually translucent to transparent on the tri-color National Line Rainbos, and opaque on the "Miller machine" tri-colors.

If the ribbons are all the same color, then the marble is referred to as a two-color National Line Rainbo. The base color can be either opaque white or an opaque color. Some of the color combinations have inspired imaginative names among collectors. Zebras are black ribbon on white base, Blue Zebras are blue ribbon on white base, Bumblebee is black ribbon on yellow base, Blue Bee is blue aventurine on yellow base, Cub Scout is yellow ribbon on blue base, Wasp is black ribbon on red base, Blue Wasp is blue ribbon on red base, Tiger is black ribbon on orange base, Blue Tiger is blue ribbon on orange base, Chocolate Cow is black ribbon on light brown base. National Line Rainbos with ribbons of two different colors are called Tri-color National Line Rainbos. They have also inspired a series of imaginative names. Ketchup

& Mustard is opaque white base with red and yellow ribbons, Christmas Tree is opaque white base with red and green ribbons, Liberty is opaque white base with red and blue ribbons. Gray-Coat is opaque white base with red and gray ribbons. Rebel is an opaque white or yellow base with black and red ribbons. Golden Rebel is opaque yellow base with red and black ribbons. Superman is opaque light blue base with yellow and red ribbons. Flaming Dragon is red and yellow on opaque green base. Blue Galaxy is red or yellow and aventurine black on light blue opaque base. Hybrid examples also exist.

The more common ribboned Peltier marble is the **Rainbo**. These are a more recent marble than the National Line Rainbo. As with the National Line Rainbo, they are a two seam design. The base glass can be a variety of opaque or transparent colors, depending on the particular type of Rainbo, and they all have a ribbon or pair of ribbons encircling the equator of the marble. There is a basic difference between a National Line Rainbo and a Rainbo. In a National Line Rainbo, the ribbons lay just on and below the surface of the marble. This is easily seen on a National Line Rainbo that has chips on the ribbons. In a Rainbo, the ribbons go into the marble towards the core.

Opaque white base with a pair of colored ribbons encircling the equator are called Rainbos. Translucent base with a pair of colored ribbons encircling the equator are called Acme Realers. An opalescent white base with a pair of red ribbons encircling the equator is called a Bloodie. A bubble-filled transparent clear base with a red and white, orange and white, or yellow and white pair of ribbons encircling the equator are called Sunsets. A transparent dark base with a yellow and white ribbon brushed on the equator of the marble is a Champion Jr. An opaque col-

ored base or transparent colored base with a pair of different colored ribbons encircling the equator are called Tri-colors. Transparent clear with ribbons of two or three different colors are called Clear Rainbos. There are also Rainbos with opaque white base and two different colors in the ribbons (similar to tri-color National Line Rainbos).

Many variations on the above basic marbles are surfacing all the time, although Rainbos do not seem to have quite the variety of Corkscrews. Some Rainbos have been found with six ribbons instead of four, and some with different colors on either side.

A number of different variations on National Line Rainbo designs and Rainbo designs have been found. Whether this indicates different machinery or just different operation of the same machine, is not known.

It should be emphasized that the ribbons on National Line Rainbos lay only on the surface or just under the surface. The ribbons on Rainbos go much farther into the marble, sometimes all the way to the center.

Peltier also produced a type of catseye. The marble consists of a single-vaned opaque color in transparent clear glass. They are referred to as **Bananas** because the shape of the vane looks like a banana. These marbles are fairly common, although not as common as other American or foreign catseyes. The most common color for the vane is yellow, red, blue, green or white. Other colors are less common. There is also a type of Peltier catseye that is similar to the Banana. These were produced only for a short period of time. They are a transparent dark amber base with a flat wide white vane in the middle. They are sometimes referred to by marble collectors as a Peltier **Root Beer Float** and have only been found in the 11/16 inch to 7/8 inch size.

Peltier Glass Company. Original Box -M. Gropper National Milkies. $1500-$2500.
Collection of Ron Simplican.

Peltier Glass Company. Assorted Slags. $10-$35 each.

Peltier Glass Company. Original Box - No. 5 National Rainbo Marbles. (Contains Slags.) $125-$250. *Collection of Darlene & Joseph Bourque.*

Peltier Glass Company. Assorted Honey Onyx. $35-$75 each.

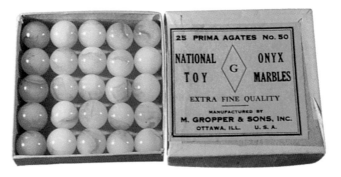

Peltier Glass Company. Original Box - M. Gropper & Sons, Prima Agates, National Onyx Toy Marbles. (Contains Honey Onyx, which may not be original to the box.) $750-$1250.

Peltier Glass Company. Assorted Peerless Patch. $2-$25 each.

Peltier Glass Company. Assorted Peerless Patch. (Pearlized.) $75-$150 each. *Collection of Cathy Runyan Svacina.*

Peltier Glass Company. Original Box - Stock Box, National Peerless. (Opalescents.) $1000-$2000. *Collection of Ron Simplican.*

Peltier Glass Company. Original Set -Picture Marbles. (Reproduction Box.) $1250-$2750. *Courtesy of Block's Box.*

Peltier Glass Company. Picture Marble - Tom Mix. $1,250-$2,500.

Peltier Glass Company. Picture Marble -Cotes Master Loaf. $900-$1500.

Peltier Glass Company. Picture Marbles, (Unusual Colors.) $500-$2,500 each.

Peltier Glass Company. Original Box - No.5, Picture Marbles. (Closed.) $500-$1000. *Courtesy of Block's Box.*

Peltier Glass Company. Picture Marbles. (Unusual Colors.) $500-$1500 each

Peltier Glass Company. Original Box - No. 5, Picture Marbles. (Open.) $500-$1000. *Courtesy of Block's Box.*

Peltier Glass Company. Original Box - 20 Picture Marbles. $1,500-$3,000. *Courtesy of Block's Box.*

Peltier Glass Company. Miller Machine Swirl. $125-$250. *Collection of Hansel deSousa.*

Peltier Glass Company. National Line Rainbo (Three Color.) Clockwise from top: Golden Rebel, Christmas Tree, Golden Rebel, Liberty, Rebel, Rebel, Ketchup and Mustard, Superman in center). $75-$1000 each. *Collection of Hansel deSousa.*

Peltier Glass Company. National Line Rainbo (Three Color.) $100-$400. *Courtesy of Block's Box.*

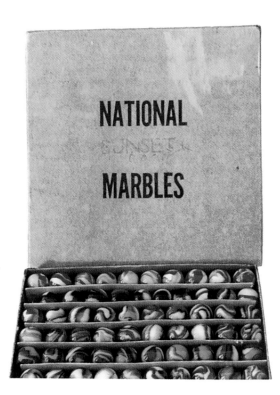

Peltier Glass Company. Original Box - Stock Box, National Line Rainbo. $5,000-$10,000. *Collection of Hansel deSousa.*

Peltier Glass Company. National Line Rainbo (Two and Three Color, Black Ribbons. First Row - Blue Galaxy. Second Row - Golden Rebel, Bumblebee. Third Row - Wasp, Zebra, Tiger). $35-$500 each.

Peltier Glass Company. National Line Rainbo. $10-$150.

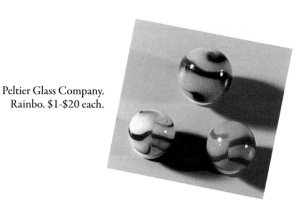

Peltier Glass Company. Rainbo. $1-$20 each.

Peltier Glass Company. National Line Rainbo (Two Color). $20-$75.

Peltier Glass Company.
Bloodies. $2-$10.

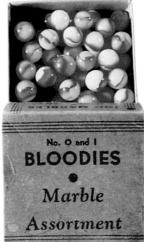

Peltier Glass Company.
Original Box - Stock Box,
Rainbos. $125-$250.

Peltier Glass
Company. Original
Box - Stock Box,
Bloodies. $150-$300.

Peltier Glass Com-
pany. Rainbos -
Experimental. $25-
$250 each.

Peltier Glass Company. Original box -M. Gropper & Sons, Prima Agates,
National Onyx Toy Marbles. (Contains Rainbos.) $150-$300.

Peltier Glass Company. Rainbo.
$1-$5 each.

Peltier Glass Com-
pany. Assorted
Rainbos. $1-$5 each.

Peltier Glass Company. Assorted Sunsets $1-$10 each.

Peltier Glass Company. Multicolor - Ribbon. $3 - $20.

Peltier Glass Company. Rainbo - Clear. $25-$75 each.

Peltier Glass Company. Assorted Champion Jr. $1-$5 each.

Peltier Glass Company. Assorted Tricolor. $1-$5 each.

Peltier Glass Company. Assorted Bananas. $1-$5 each.

Peltier Glass Company. Multicolor - Swirl. $10-$50 each.

Peltier Glass Company. Assorted "Root Beer Floats." $60-$125 each.

Peltier Glass Company. Original Boxes - M. Gropper Prima Agates (left), M. Gropper National Prima (fight). $100-$800 each. *Collection of Darlene & Joseph Bourrque.*

Peltier Glass Company. Original Box - Gift Set, M. Gropper No. 28 Lucky Boy Champion Marble Set. (Open, National Line Rainbos.) $1000-$2000.

Peltier Glass Company. Original Box - Stock Box, Black Opaque. $100-$200.

Peltier Glass Company. Original Box - Gift Set, M. Gropper No. 28 Lucky Boy Champion Marble Set. (Closed.) $200-$400.

Peltier Glass Company. Original Box - Gift Set, M. Gropper No. 28 Lucky Boy Champion Marble Set. (Open, Slags.) $275-$550.

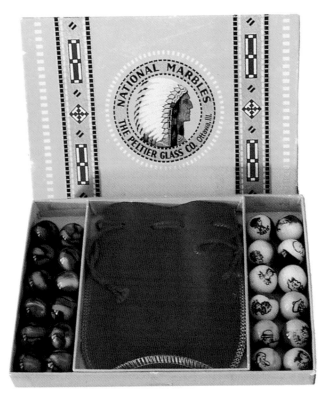

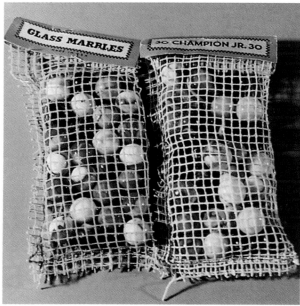

Peltier Glass Company. Original Box - Mesh Bag, Champion Jr. (Contains Rainbos.) $30-$60.

Peltier Glass Company. Original Box - Gift Box, National Marbles "Indian Head." $5,000-$10,000. *Collection of Hansel deSousa.*

(HS)Peltier Glass Company. Original Bag - National Rainbo Agates (Gropper, Originally a Gift Set). $50-$100. *Collection of Harold Sugerman.*

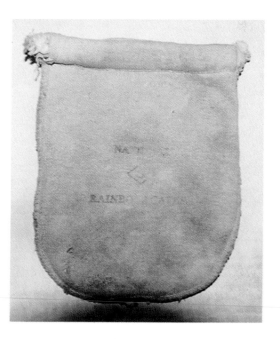

Peltier Glass Company. Original Box - Gift Box. (Stained Glass Design.) $3,500-$7,000. *Collection of Anonymous.*

Peltier Glass Company. Original Printing Block - National Marbles (Used for Brochures and Advertisements). $150-$300. *Courtesy of Block's Box.*

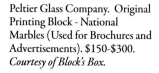

Peltier Glass Company. Original Jewelry - contains Peerless Patches. $15-$30.

THE MASTER MARBLE COMPANY/THE MASTER GLASS COMPANY

The Master Marble Company was founded in 1930 by four former employees of the Akro Agate Company. The company closed in 1941 and the machinery was purchased by one of the former owners, Clinton F. Israel, who formed The Master Glass Company. Master Glass subsequently closed in 1973. In 1952, Clinton Israel purchased most of the assets of the Akro Agate Company, including unsold marbles and packaging.

The Master Marble Company used machinery which was similar to Akro Agate's, but most notably, did not include the Freese improvement which offset the rollers. Because of this, Master marbles have a crimp or feathering mark at either pole. Also, due to the design of the machinery, Master marbles have a unique pattern at either end. You can see a small "V" of the color on one side of the marble indenting into the color on the other side.

The most collectible Master marble is the **Sunburst**, and a related marble called the **Tigereye**. The Sunburst was an attempt to duplicate handmade Onionskins, as well as Akro Agate Sparklers. The marble is a transparent clear base with filaments and strands of various colors running from pole to pole and completely filling the marble. Some Sunbursts have clear patches or areas in them. A Tigereye is a Sunburst that is almost completely clear. It has filaments and strands forming a wide, flat ribbon in the center of the marble. They are much less common than Sunbursts. The colors are usually orange, white, and black in a transparent clear base.

Master Marble also made some patch marbles that are collectible. These patches were marketed under a variety of names, including **Meteor** (wispy translucent patch on opaque base), **Comet** (opaque patch on opaque base), and **Cloudy** (translucent patch on translucent base). The Master Marble patches are identifiable by a "V" or "U" pattern and feathering visible at each pole. The patches were made in a variety of patterns, including two-color opaque, two-color translucent, and opaque with a second color brushed on. Master Marbles' colors are fairly unique, although generally duller than Akro's.

Master Marble and Master Glass made a variety of **clearies**, **opaques**, and **catseyes** (Master Glass only). Master clearies and opaques all have the typical

"V" or "U" pattern at either end. Master catseyes are typically single color translucent three or four vane variety in transparent clear glass.

Master Marble Company. Assorted Sunbursts (Opaque). $3-$75 each.

Master Marble Company. Assorted Sunbursts (Clear, first two marbles in row 2 are Tigereyes). $5-$75.

Master Marble Company. Original Box - Stock Box, Sunbursts (Open). $500-$1000

Master Marble Company. Assorted Cloudies. $1-$5 each.

Master Marble Company. Original Box - Stock Box, Comets (On End Flap). $300-$600. *Courtesy of Block's Box.*

MASTER MADE MARBLES

Master Marble Company. Original Box - Stained Glass Design, Contains Cloudies. $200-$400.

Master Marble Company. Original Box - Display Box, Comets (Closed). $300-$600.

Master Marble Company. Assorted Meteors. $1-$5 each.

Master Marble Company. Assorted Comets. $1-$5 each.

Master Marble Company. Original Box - Display Box, Comets (Open). $300-$600.

Master Marble Company. Original Box - "Bulls-Eye" (contains Comets). $300-$600.

Master Marble Company. Premium - Comets in Cellophane Tubes (Used as Giveaways). $30-$60. *Collection of Darlene & Joseph Bourque.*

Master Marble Company. Original Boxes - Marble Shooters. $150-$500 each. *Collection of Hansel deSousa.*

Master Marble Company. Original Boxes - Century of Progress (Small and Medium Sizes, with Original Wrappers). $1000-$3000. *Collection of Hansel deSousa.*

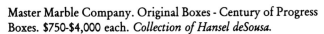
Master Marble Company. Original Boxes - Century of Progress Boxes. $750-$4,000 each. *Collection of Hansel deSousa.*

Master Marble Company. Original Box - College Collection (Closed). $1,000-$2,000 each. *Collection of Hansel deSousa.*

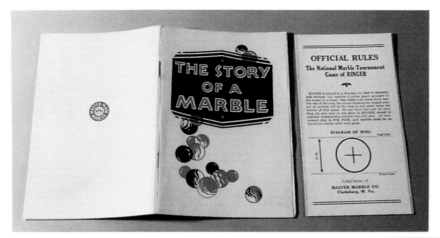

Master Marble Company. Original Booklet - The Story of A Marble and Official Rules of Ringer (Included in Some Century of Progress Boxes). $75-$150.

Master Marble Company. Original Box - "Sun-Beam" (Medium Size) (Closed). $400-$800. *Collection of Darlene & Joseph Bourque.*

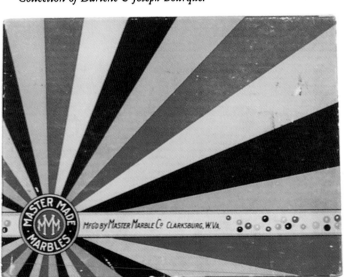

Master Marble Company. Original Box - College Collection (Open). $1,000-$2,000 each. *Collection of Hansel deSousa.*

Master Marble Company. Original Boxes - Century of Progress Box, Contains a Hand-cut Agate. $450-$900.

Bottom left: Master Marble Company. Original Boxes - "Sun-Beam" (Small and Medium Size). $300-$800. *Collection of Hansel deSousa.*

Bottom right: Master Marble Company. Original Box - "Sun-Beam" (Medium Size) (Open). $400-$800. *Collection of Darlene & Joseph Bourque.*

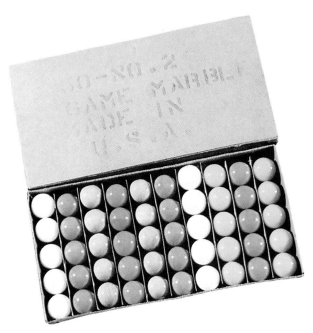

Master Marble Company. Original Box -Game Marbles (Stenciled). $250-$500. *Courtesy of Block's Box.*

Master Marble Company. Original Box - Game Marble Set. $250-$500

Master Marble Company. Original Box - Display Box, Opals (Closed). $300-$600.

Master Marble Company. Original Box - No. 130 (part of a Game Marble Set). $25-$50

Master Marble Company. Original Box - Display Box, Opals (Open). $300-$600.

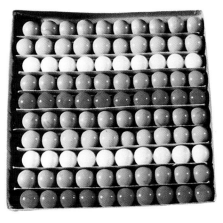

Master Marble Company. Original Box - No. 113 "Sun-Beam," (Top is plain, bottom is a Promotional Box). $75-$150

Master Glass Company. Original Box - No. 5 $10-$20 (empty), $25-$50 (full).

Master Glass Company. Original Box - Bullseye (Small). $300-$600. *Courtesy of Block's Box.*

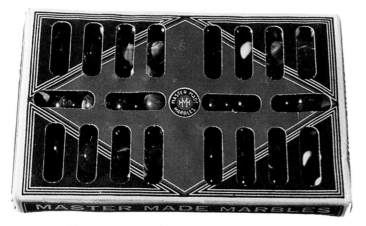

Master Marble Company. Original Box -No. 10 (Top). $75-$150.

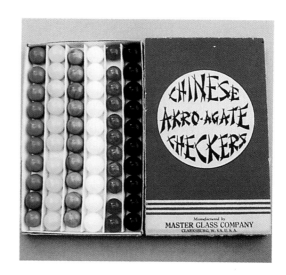

Master Glass Company. Original Box - Akro Agate Chinese Checkers (Multicolor Box). $100-$200. *Collection of Darlene & Joseph Bourque.*

Master Marble Company. Original Box - No. 10 (bottom) $75-$150.

Master Glass Company. Original Bag - Poly Bag of Catseyes. $10-$20.

MARBLE KING, INC.

Marble King was started in 1949 by Berry Pink and Sellers Peltier in St. Mary's, West Virginia. It was moved to Paden City, West Virginia, in 1958 after a fire destroyed the original plant. Berry Pink had also been jobbing marbles since the 1920s under the trade name "Berry Pink, Inc."

Marble King produced ribboned, patch and ribbon, catseye, and swirl marbles. Patch and ribbon marbles have a patch on one pole, a ribbon of a second color encircling the marble, a ribbon of the same color as the top patch encircling the marble and finally a patch of the second color on the bottom pole. The marbles have two seams. They are made using a veneering method which puts a thin layer of the colored glass on a base of white glass. These marbles were marketed under the name **"Rainbows."**

The most common Rainbow is white alternating with a second color. The second color is usually red, blue, brown, or green. There are Rainbows that are white with a color ribbon and patch consisting of two or three different colors. These are rarer. The most collectible Rainbows are two different alternating colors (not white). These have imaginative names given to them by collectors. In ascending order of rarity they are: Bumblebee (yellow and black), Wasp (red and black), Cub Scout (blue and yellow), Girl Scout (green and yellow), Tiger (orange and yellow), Spiderman (red and blue), Green Hornet (green and black), Watermelon (red and green), and Dragonfly (green and blue). There are also hybrid examples that are either a Patch or consist of three or four colors. These are very rare. Spidermen, Green Hornets, Watermelons, and Dragonflies have only been found in

the 5/8 inch size. Girl Scouts and Tigers have only been found up to 3/4 inch. Larger examples (up to 1 inch) exist of the other marble types. Vintage patch and ribbon Rainbows were produced until the early 1970s, although it seems that the two-color variety were not produced much past the mid-1960s.

Some experimental Marble King Rainbows have surfaced that have a completely transparent clear base with one color patch and ribboned on the surface. Also, a very large number of hybrid type Rainbows have surfaced in the last decade as numerous dump sites have been excavated.

Another collectible Marble King marble is the **Rainbow Red**. This is a white base marble with an equatorial ribbon of red and a second equatorial ribbon of a different color, rather than a patch.

There are several types of new marbles being produced, or that have been recently produced, that are very similar to vintage Rainbows in terms of color and pattern. These include Rainbow-looking marbles that have a translucent base, Rainbow-looking marbles that are missing the patch but have the equatorial ribbon, Rainbows that have two patches, but no ribbon, and Rainbow-looking marbles where the two colors are blended together in thin strands or bands. These have all been produced since the mid-1970s, and blended Rainbows were produced for a limited time in 1995.

Marble King, Inc. Original Box - Chinese Checkers (Chinko-Checko-Marblo), Peltier (top), Berry Pink, Inc. (bottom). $25-$150 each. *Courtesy of A Chip Off the Old Block.*

Marble King Inc. Original Box - Champion Set (Berry Pink, Inc.). $150-$300.

Marble King, Inc. Original Game - Chinese Checkers (Chinko-Checko-Marblo) $30-$60. *Courtesy of A Chip Off the Old Block.*

Marble King Inc. Assorted Rainbows (Multicolor with White). 50¢-$1.

Marble King Inc. Original Box - Chinese Checkers (Berry Pink, Inc.). $20-$40.

Marble King Inc. Rainbow (Multicolor with White). 50¢-$1.

Marble King Inc. Assorted Rainbows (Two Color) (First Row - Dragonfly, Watermelon, Spiderman, Spidermelon. Second Row - Green Hornet, Ruby Bee, Tiger. Third Row - Girl Scout, Cub Scout, Wasp, Bumblebee). $2-$1,000 each.

Marble King Inc. Assorted Rainbows. (Two Color, White). 25¢-50¢. *Courtesy of A Chip Off the Old Block.*

Marble King Inc. Assorted Rainbow Reds. 25¢-50¢.

Marble King Inc.
Patch - Spiderman
Patch. $125-$250.

Marble King, Inc. Cats-
eye -St. Mary's $15-$75.

Marble King, Inc. Original Bag - Tournament Assortment.
(Poly.) $10-$20 (empty, $15-$150 (full).

Marble King Inc.
Original Bag - Mesh Bag.
(Contains Peltier
Rainbos.) $75-$150.

Marble King, Inc. Original Bag - Poly. (Rainbows, Rainbow Reds,
Cat's Eyes) $5-$100.

Marble King, Inc. Original Bag - Mesh Bags, Morton Salt Advertiser,
(Contains Peltier Rainbos.) $40-$80.

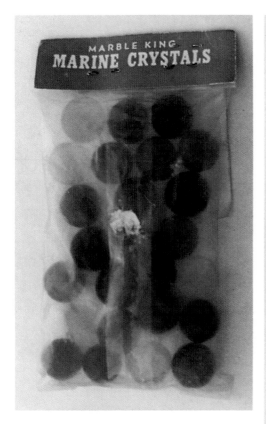

Marble King Inc. Original Bag - Marine
Crystals, Poly. $10-$20.

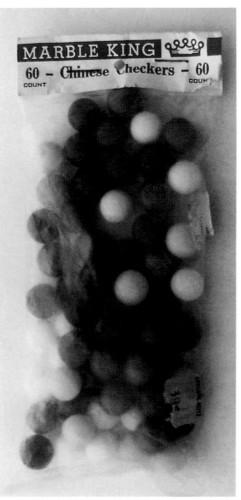

Marble King, Inc. Original Bag - Chinese Checkers.
Poly. $5-$15.

Marble King, Inc. Original Bag - Cat's Eyes.
Poly. $2.50-$10.

Marble King, Inc. Original Bag - Bowlers.
(Cat's Eyes.) Poly. $5-$10.

Marble King, Inc. Original Blister Pack.
(Post-1975 Patches.) $2.50-$5.

VITRO AGATE COMPANY/ GLADDING-VITRO AGATE COMPANY

The Vitro Agate Company began operations in 1932 in Parkersburg, West Virginia. It was acquired in 1969 by The Gladding Corporation, which changed the name to Gladding-Vitro Agate Company. In 1982, Gladding-Vitro was purchased by Paris Manufacturing Company, which changed the name back to Vitro Agate. In 1987, it was purchased by Viking Rope Company which retained the name, but moved the company to Anacortes, Washington. The company ceased operations in 1993. The machinery and name were purchased by JABO, Inc. and the company known as JABO-Vitro Agate Company.

Early Vitro Agate marbles are the brushed variety. This type has a thin layer of colored glass brushed on a base color. There are also a few veneered varieties, but these were manufactured in later years.

More recently, Vitro Agate also made some two-seam marbles that are similar to Marble King Rainbows. They are readily identifiable because the marbles always have a defined crimp design at the seam between the two halves. Marble King marbles do not have this crimp. Vitro also produced a number of two-seam multicolor patch marbles. Many of these have clear and wispy white as one of the colors. When viewed ninety degrees from the seam, many have a stylized "V" pattern.

A **Victory** is a transparent clear base with an opaque color patch brushed on about a quarter of the surface. The patch is purple, green, yellow, blue or red. The **Conqueror** is more common than the Victory. It has a transparent clear base with the same type of patch as the Victory, however, the remainder of the marble is brushed with opaque white. These marbles are usually found in 5/8 inch, but examples up to 15/16 inch are known to exist. There are two other marbles, similar to a Conqueror. One looks just like a Conqueror, but most of the interior of the marble is filled with translucent white filaments (occasionally the marble is opalescent). These are often referred to as **"Phantom Conquerors."** They are much more common than the Conqueror and are least collectible at this time. The other type is very similar to a Conqueror, but has a brushed white that is more off-white than a Conqueror and a colored patch that is not as bright.

Another type of Vitro Agate that is collectible was marketed as **Blackies** and **Whities**. Blackies are opaque white with a black band around the equator and a colored brushed patch on either pole. Whities are opaque white with a translucent color band around the equator. A slightly more recent Vitro Agate is **All-Reds**. All-Reds come in two varieties. The older variety is an opaque white base with a red patch on one pole and a different color on the other. There is a black line encircling the red patch. The other type of All-Red, which is newer, has a red patch on one pole and a color patch on the other, with no black line.

Vitro Agate also produced another type of brushed opaque marble called the **"Parrot,"** that has recently become collectible. This is a white base marble that has four patches of color. The patches can be blue, purple, black, yellow, or aventurine green.

Vitro Parrots, as well as other Vitro swirls sometimes have a "V" pattern in the glass. This design make was intentional.

Vitro Agate made a variety of other transparent and opaque marbles, as well as catseyes. The Vitro Agate tri-color patch is a transparent clear base marble with four different colored patches brushed on the surface. Vitro Agate also produced some catseyes that are beginning to become collectible. Vitro Agate Catseyes are either a four or five wavy vane type. Gladding-Vitro Catseyes are a five to eight strand cage style. Some cage styles can be found in aqua glass. There are some Vitro Agate vane-style Catseyes that have two or more colors on each vane. These are referred to as hybrids, although they seem to be too common to have been an accident.

Vitro Agate Company. Original Bag- Poly. $5-$20 (Empty), $20-$60 (Full).

Vitro Agate Company. Original Bag - Conquerors. $30-$60.

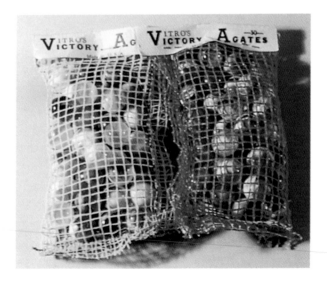

Vitro Agate Company. Original Bag - Mesh, Victory Agates. $30-$60.

Vitro Agate Company. Original Game - Includes Conquerors. $150-$300. Collection of Hansel deSousa.

Vitro Agate Company. Brushed - (First Row - Victory. Second Row - Conqueror, "Phantom" Conqueror). 10¢-$1 each.

Vitro Agate Company. Original Bag - Mesh. (Contains Brushed Patches.) $15-$30.

Vitro Agate Company. Original Box - Gift Set. (Contains Brushed Patches.) $400-$800. Collection of David Freburg.

Vitro Agate Company. Original Bag - Poly. (Bottle Hanger Advertiser.) (Contains Brushed Patches.) $25-$50.

Vitro Agate Company. Brushed Patch - Oxblood. $50-$100.

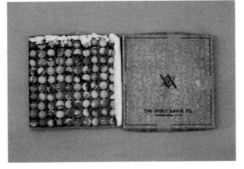

Vitro Agate Company. Original Box -Stock Box. (Wood Grain Cover, contains Brushed Tri-color.) $350-$700. *Courtesy of Block's Box.*

Vitro Agate Company. Assorted Brushed Patch. 50 cents -$5.

Vitro Agate Company. Original Bags - Poly. (Contain Brushed Tri-Colors.) $10-$20.

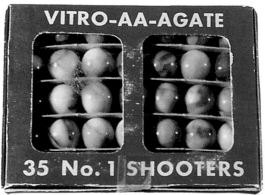

Vitro Agate Company. Original Box - Cellophane Panel. (Contains Brushed Tri-Colors.) $200-$400.

Vitro Agate Company. Assorted Patch, Parrots. $50-$200 each.

Vitro Agate Company. Assorted Brushed Tri-color. 50¢-$2 each.

Vitro Agate Company. Assorted Patch. 25¢-$1 each.

Vitro Agate Company. Ribboned - Whitie (left), Blackie (right). $1-$5 each.

Vitro Agate Company. Original Box - Salesman's Sample Kit. $1000-$2000.
Collection of David Freburg.

Vitro Agate Company. Assorted Patch, Excellent "V"s. $50-$100 each.

Vitro Agate Company. Assorted All-Red. 10¢-50¢ each.

Vitro Agate Company. Original Bag - All Reds, Poly. (White Label). (Black Line marbles on left, No Line marbles on right.) $10-$20 each.

Vitro Agate Company. Original Bag - All Reds, Poly. (Red Label.) $10-$20.

Vitro Agate Company. Original Sleeve - Cellophane Sleeve of Hybrid Catseyes, Premium in Bread and Cereal. $10-$20.

Vitro Agate Company. Original Bag - Catseyes Hybrids, Poly. (Red Label.) $15-$30.

Gladding-Vitro. Original Bag - All Reds, Poly. $10-$20.

Vitro Agate Company. Original Bag - Catseyes, Poly. (Red Label.) $10-$20.

Vitro Agate Company. Original Bag - Chinese Checkers. $15-$40.

Vitro Agate Company. Original Bags - Poly. Chinese Checkers (left), Catseyes (right) (White Label). $5-$20.

Vitro Agate Company. Original Game - Circle-X. $50-$100.

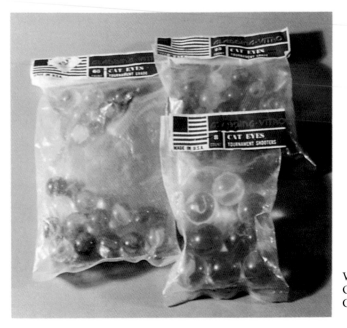

Vitro Agate Company. Original Bag - Poly, Exotic Glass Gem. (White Label). $10-$20.

Vitro Agate Company. Original Bags -Poly. Catseyes. $5-$20.

Vitro Agate Company. Original Bag - All Reds, Poly. (Red Label.) $15-$30.

Vitro Agate Company. Original Bag - Swirl, poly. (Last Bag Made by Company.) $10-$20.

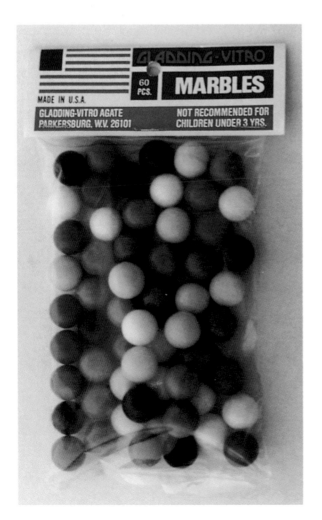

JABO-Vitro Agate Company. Assorted Classics. 25 cents -$5.

Gladding-Vitro Agate Company. Original Bag - Poly. Chinese Checkers. $5-$15.

RAVENSWOOD
NOVELTY WORKS

The Ravenswood Novelty Company began operations during 1931 or 1932, under the guidance of John Turnbull. Operations ended around 1954 or 1955, although the company is reported to have made industrial marbles through 1959. During the late 1950s, Ravenswood was a major supplier of marbles to Krylon Paint for aerosol cans. It is believed they purchased these marbles from Vitro Agate Company.

The company made **Transparent** and **Opaque Swirls**. There is also strong evidence to suggest that they made the 1 inch Buddy marbles and did not buy them from Master Glass, as had been previously believed.

Ravenswood swirls are very unique in terms of coloring and design. Ravenswood generally produced marbles in the 9/16 inch to 5/8 inch size.

Ravenswood Novelty Works. Original Box - Buddy. $40-$60.
Courtesy of A Chip Off the Old Block.

Ravenswood Novelty Works. Assorted Swirls. $1-$10 each.
Collection of David Chamberlain.

Ravenswood Novelty Works. Original Bag - Buddy. Mesh.
$10-$25.

Ravenswood Novelty
Works. Assorted Swirls.
$1-$10 each. *Collection
of David Chamberlain.*

ALLEY AGATE COMPANY

Lawrence Alley operated factories in at least four different locations in West Virginia (Paden City, Sisterville, Pennsboro, and St. Mary's) between 1929 and 1949. Some believe that he purchased Christensen Agates's Machinery. It is believed he may also have operated a plant in Salem, West Virginia. In 1949, he sold the St. Mary's plant to Berry Pink and Sellers Peltier, and they changed the company name to Marble King.

Alley produced a large variety of two and three color **Swirls**, as well as one color opaques and clearies. They also produced a very small size marble, 3/8 inch in diameter. Additional future research is required in order to positively identify the unique marbles that Alley made. It is known that Alley produced marbles using a metallic color, as well as an oxblood, and he produced sets of children's dishes, similar to those made by Akro, including the Orphan Annie sets.

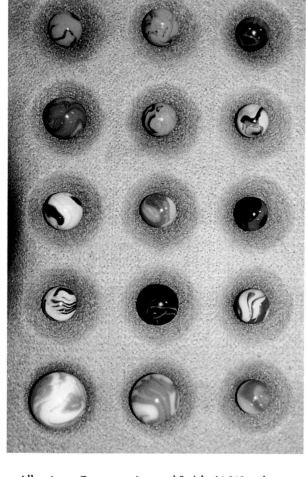

Alley Agate Company. Assorted Swirls. $1-$10 each. *Collection of David Chamberlain.*

Alley Agate Company. Assorted Swirls. $1-$10 each. *Collection of David Chamberlain.*

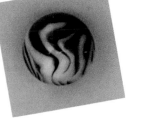

Alley Agate Company. Flame Swirl. $10-$25 each. *Courtesy of Block's Box.*

Alley Agate Company. Original Box - Allies, J. Pressman. $20-$40.

Alley Agate Company. Original Box - Allies, J. Pressman. $20-$40.

ALOX MANUFACTURING COMPANY

The Alox Manufacturing Company began operations in the early 1920s in St. Louis, Missouri. The company produced **Opaque** marbles, **Two-Color Swirls**, and a **Transparent Swirl**. There has been additional research which has now identified a number of different swirls with Alox Manufacturing. The company appears to have made marbles limited to 5/8 inch in diameter.

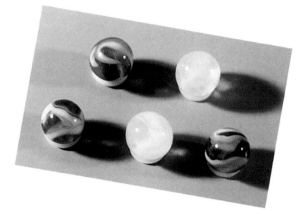

Alox Manufacturing Company. Assorted Transparent Swirls. 25¢-$1 each.

Alox Manufacturing Company. Original Bag - Mesh Bag, Swirls. $30-$60.

Alox Manufacturing Company. Original Game - Tit-Tat-Toe. $25-$50.

CHAMPION AGATE COMPANY

The Champion Agate Company began operations in Pennsboro, West Virgina, in 1938, and are still producing marbles. The company only produces **Swirls**. They are about 5/8 inch in diameter. In the early 1980s, the company produced a series of marbles that are similar to two-color and three-color swirls produced during the 1930s. They also produced a marble that looks like a Wire Pull. These marbles are referred to as "New Old-Fashioneds." They are often mistaken for older Swirls. Because they have a very shiny or oily surface to them the difference is noticeable

Champion Agate Company. Assorted Swirls. (First Row, Second Marble is A New Old-Fashioned). 10¢-50¢ each.

Champion Agate Company. Original Bag - Assorted, Poly. $5-$10.
Collection of Les Jones.

CAIRO NOVELTY COMPANY

The Cairo Novelty Company began operations in 1948 in Cairo, West Virginia. With the financial backing of two local merchants, John Sandy and Dennis Farley, Cairo had been formed late in the prior year by Oris Hanlon, who had left Heaton Agate Company. The company had only one marble machine, but a design innovation by Hanlon, which is patented, allowed it to produce marbles at a fifty percent faster rate than any other machine in operation at the time. The company produced a wide variety of **swirls** from peewee size to 3/4 inch. Many of these marbles fluoresce. Their major account was Woolworth's Five and Ten Cent Stores, and they packaged mesh bags with the Woolworth's label on them. Cairo also marketed marbles in boxes with their own name. Both of these original packages are hard to find. The company also produced and marketed a game called "Trap the Fox" in the late 1940s. The game included black and white swirls (the hounds) and an opaque marble (the fox). A flash flood in 1950 seriously curtailed operations, but Cairo was able to produce marbles until 1953. Further research needs to be done in order to identify the marbles that were specifically made by this plant.

Cairo Novelty Company. Assorted Swirls. $1-$10 each.

HEATON AGATE COMPANY/C.E. BOGARD & SONS/THE BOGARD COMPANY/JABO, INC./ JABO-VITRO AGATE, INC.

Heaton Agate Company. Original Box - "Big Shot." J. Pressman, Swirls. $20-$40 each.

The Heaton Agate Company began operations in 1946-1947 in Pennsboro, West Virginia. It was originally run by Bill Heaton and Oris Hanlon. Hanlon left the company in 1947 to found the Cairo Novelty Company. Until the early 1960s, the company produced a variety of **Opaque Swirls** and **Transparent Swirls**, as well as **Catseyes** and **Game Marbles**. During the 1960s, production of swirls ceased and the company restricted itself to producing Catseyes and industrial marbles. It is reported that Heaton possessed a 3/8 inch marble making machine and produced 3/8 inch Catseyes. Research continues in the area of identifying specific swirl patterns and catseyes that were made by the company.

C.E. Bogard bought the Heaton Agate Company in 1971 and renamed it the C.E. Bogard & Sons Company. In 1983 the company name was changed to The Bogard Company by Clayton Bogard's son, Jack. Bogard produced a variety of Catseyes, Clearies, and Opaques. According to Jack Bogard, the company also produced an experimental marble (transparent clear base with interior green wisps) that can be found in the Mountaineer blister packs the company marketed.

JABO, Inc., was organized in 1987 by Jack Bogard, Dave McCullough (who had spent many years at Champion Agate), and Joanne Argabrite. The machinery was moved to Reno, Ohio. The company produced industrial marbles, mainly Opaques. However, Dave McCullough would produce three or four limited runs each year of **"Classics"** in sizes from 5/8 inch to 1 inch. Each run was different from any previous run, and the marbles were not like any other company's. Many fluoresce, and contain many innovative colors which were produced in very short runs.

In early 1996, JABO, Inc. bought Vitro Agate Company, moving the Vitro machinery from Anacortes, Washington, to the Reno, Ohio, location. JABO, Inc. was reorganized as JABO-Vitro Agate Company. The company now produces a wide variety of Swirl marbles.

Heaton Agate Company. Original Bag - Royal Immies. $75-$150.
Courtesy of A Chip Off the Old Block.

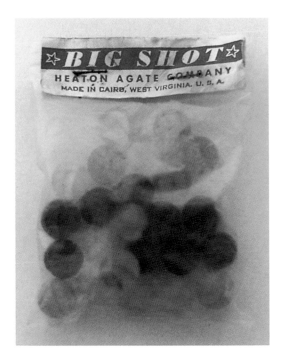

Heaton Agate Company. Original Bag - "Big Shot," Catseyes, Poly. $10-$20.

C. E. Bogard & Sons. Original Bag - Catsyeys, Poly. $5-$20.

MISCELLANEOUS MACHINE MADE MARBLES

Marbles with metallic stripes have been made by several manufacturers, including Alley Agate, Vitro Agate, and Champion Agate. Usually, they have a silvery stripe on the colored swirl of a common swirl marble. Occasionally, you will find a silver stripe on a Clearie or a copper colored stripe on a Swirl.

Marbles with **Aventurine** in them have become popular recently. The aventurine is actually finely ground metal flecks mixed in with the glass. Aventurine is sometimes found in the black ribbons and patches on Peltier National Line Rainbos and Peerless Patches. It has also been found in common Swirls with green swirls on white. It is not known who made these marbles. Aventurine has also been found in some Vitro Agate Ribboned Marbles. These always have an opaque white base with at least one green ribbon. Also, some Vitro Agate four-vane Catseyes have been found with aventurine in them. The vanes are usually green and these usually have a lot of "fire" in them. Marble King Rainbos will contain some large aventurine flakes on occasion

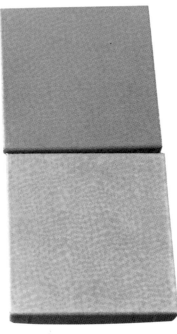

Other. Assorted Jobber Boxes. $50-$150 each.

Other. Assorted Jobber boxes. (Stained Glass, Bottom is Akro Agate,) $75-$450.

Other. Original Blister Pack - Steelie Marbles.
$15-$30.

Other. Original Box - Sureshot Glass Marbles, J. Pressman. (Contains Heaton Agates.)
$100-$200. *Collection of Darlene & Joseph Bourque.*

Other. Original Box -
Star Chinese Check-
ers, L. G. Ballard Mfg.
Co. $30-$60.

Other. Assorted Metallic Marbles. $1-$25 each.

Other. Original Bag - Chinese Checkers,
Stevens Mfg. Co. $5-$15.

Other. Assorted Aventurine Marbles. $5-$35 each.

Other. Original Bag - labeled ELCEEBEE International, Boston, Made in Japan. (Knockoff of Marble King Bag.) $30-$60.

Other. Original Box - Tournament Glass Marbles, The Rosenthal Co. (Contains Master Marble Cloudies.) $250-$500. *Collection of Lefty Bingham.*

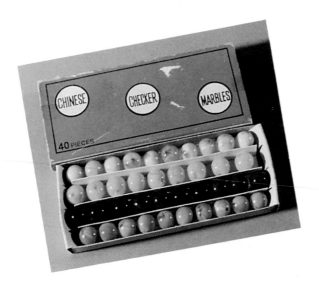

Chinese Checkers. Original Box - Japan. (40-count and 60- count) $15-$75

Other. Original Box - Japan, Transparent Swirl $50-$100. *Collection of Hansel deSousa.*

CATSEYES

Virtually every manufacturer, since the late 1940s, has made catseye marbles. The majority of Catseye marbles are foreign-made.

The first American Catseyes were manufactured by Peltier Glass Company. This is the **Peltier Banana**. Bananas are opaque single vane Catseyes with occasionally slight ridges in transparent clear glass. The next American manufacturer of catseyes appears to have been Master Glass Company. These are three- or four-vane translucent Catseyes in transparent clear glass. Another early Catseye is the Marble King St. Mary's. This is a four vane Catseye with one vane plane in one color and the other vane plane in another color.

Catseyes were also made by **Vitro Agate (four and five vane)**, **Gladding-Vitro (cage style)**, and a number of later manufacturers.

Foreign Catseyes continue to be made in Mexico and the Far East. Most of these are single color four vane, or three color six vane. The glass of many foreign Catseyes has a light bottle green tint to it.

There is still much research that needs to be done into catseye marbles, but some of these are beginning to become quite collectible, something that many collectors would have laughed at several years ago.

Catseyes. Foreign Catseyes. 10¢ to $5 each.

Catseyes. Nine-vane Catseyes. $10-$100 each.

Catseyes. American Catseyes (First Row - Marble King St. Mary's. Second Row - Vitro Agate, Heaton Agate. Third Row - Gladding Vitro, Marble King, Gladding Vitro).

Catseyes. Original Bag - Santa's Marbles. $10-$20.

Catseyes. Original Bag - Uncle Jack's Poly. (Note Catseye Marble in the label.) $25-$50.

Catseyes. Original Bag - China. $1-$5.

Catseyes. Original Bag - Sun Brand (left), Camel (right), Poly. Japan. $10-$30.

Catseyes. Original Blister Packs- China (Bozo the Clown, Bullwinkle.) $2.50-$10.

Catseyes. Original Box - Camel, Japan. $30-$60.

Catseyes. Original Box - Japan. $15-$35.

EUROPEAN MACHINE-MADE MARBLES

Machine made marbles that were manufactured in Europe have begun to be identified by collectors. There are several types of marbles that have been positively identified as coming from Europe. The first is the **"Foreign Sparkler."** These have appeared in two versions; the faded pastel color, and a more colorful version. The faded pastel type appears to be of more recent vintage than the brighter type, and appears to have been made by a different manufacturer. The "bright" type has a thin vane in the center with assorted bright colors on it. The poles exhibit the "V" or "U" pattern similar to Master Marbles. I have only seen it in sizes between 19/32 inch and 23/32 inch. It is believed these marbles are from the 1940s or 1950s. Along with loose examples, there have been examples of embedded marbles in a bar of soap shaped like a little girl. One of the bars of soap was a in a box indicating it had been manufactured in France, and an example that is printed with the name "Bonux," a French soap, on it has been identified. The "faded pastel" type has a wide vane that fills the marble. The surface has an "orange peel" texture and usually has creases at the seam lines. This marble may actually be Vacor de Mexico. They are usually found about 1 inch in diameter.

Another type of European marble is a **Wire Pull**. These have been found in a multitude of sizes, base colors and wire colors. Wire Pulls consist of a transparent base (filled with air bubbles) and a continuous "wire" of color (or two wires of different colors). The "wire" is uniform in width throughout the marble. It is most likely that they were manufactured in West Germany, possibly in the 1960s.

A marble referred to as the **"Spaghetti Swirl"** appears to be from the same manufacturer as the Wire Pull. These have been found with groups of Wire Pulls. They are found in a transparent colored base with opaque swirls or opaque base with transparent swirls.

The only other machine made marbles known to have been manufactured in Europe are a small group of **Corkscrew-style** marbles that were made in Czechoslovakia. This small group was found in Europe, and were reportedly manufactured in the 1930s. There were two different types found. One is a Corkscrew type that is transparent clear on one side and transparent Vaseline yellow on the other. The other is a Corkscrew consisting of tiny pieces of colored glass, much like Guinea flecks, in transparent clear.

No doubt additional European marbles will continue to surface as the hobby develops outside of the United States.

Foreign. Assorted European Spaghetti Swirl. $5-$25 each. Left: *Courtesy of Dessarae Rhyn.*

Foreign. Assorted European Wire Pull. $5-$25 each.

Foreign. Assorted Foreign Sparklers. (Top is Mexican "Pastel" type, Bottom are European "Bright" type.) $5-$25 each.

Foreign. Assorted Czechoslovakia Corkscrews. Too Rare to Value.

VACOR DE MEXICO

Vacor de Mexico is a Mexican manufacturer of marbles. The company began operations sometime in the 1930s and is today one of the largest, if not the largest, manufacturer of marbles in the world. Their marbles are marketed under a variety of imaginative names: **Pirate**, **Galaxy**, **Meteor**, **Galacticas**, **Silver**, **Agate**. They are readily identifiable based on two features. First, the marbles tend to have an oily or iridescent sheen to them. Second, the glass tends to have ripples and creases in the surface. Many of the marbles found in toy stores today are made by Vacor de Mexico.

Foreign. Original Bag - Poly Mesh. Vacor de Mexico. $1-$5.

Foreign. Vacor de Mexico. 1 cent to $1 each.

Foreign. Original box - Vacor de Mexico. $2.50-$10.

Foreign. Original Blister Pack - Poly Mesh. Vacor de Mexico. $1-$5.

COMMON MACHINE MADE MARBLES

There are literally millions of machine made marbles in existence. It has been reported that some companies were able to produce several boxcar loads of marbles a day. Most of these were Game Marbles (Opaques), Catseyes, Swirls, and Patches.

Almost every machine made marble produced after 1950 can be found in abundant quantities and have colors which are dull and patterns which are non-descript, and therefore have no eye appeal.

The lack of color and pattern is not an accident. As the toy marble market matured, it became imperative for manufacturers to cut costs as low as possible in order to compete. One way to do this was to eliminate the expensive materials that it took to produce bright colors and eliminate the inefficient machinery that it took to produce interesting patterns.

Over ninety percent of the Machine made marbles that you run across will not match any of the marbles described above. This does not mean they are not collectible. There is an almost endless variation of colors and design. Some collectors enjoy putting together collections of these marbles in odd colors and designs, specifically because they are shunned by the larger majority of collectors.

Do not toss these marbles aside, just because they are common. There are many young children who still enjoy playing with marbles and who are not interested in their value. Consider "recycling" your marbles with a local Cub Scout troop (they can get an achievement pin for learning to play marbles), or a local school or other club. The looks on the kids' faces when you give them your bulk marbles is worth a thousand times more than the value of the marbles you are giving away.

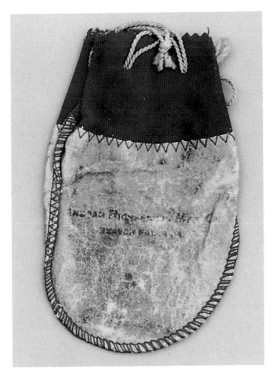

Advertising. Advertising Marble Bag - Ingram Richman Mfg. $75-$150. *Collection of Lefty Bingham.*

Advertising. Cardboard Sleeve - Robin Hood Shoes. $100-$200. *Courtesy of Block's Box.*

Advertising. Advertising Bag - Worcester Salt, Mesh. $50-$100. *Courtesy of Block's Box.*

Advertising. Advertising Marbles - Goodrich and Ingram Richman Mfg. $75-$300 each. *Collection of Lefty Bingham.*

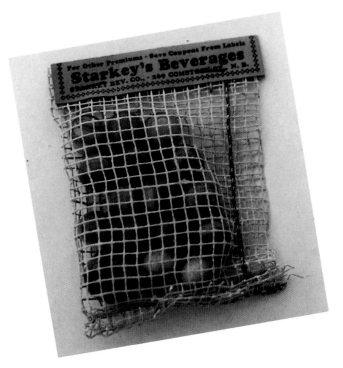

Advertising. Advertising Bag - Starkey's Beverages (front), mesh. $35-$75.

Advertising. Bottle Hanging Bag - Cott's, Poly. $25-$50.

Advertising. Advertising Bag -Starkey's Beverages (back) mesh. $35-$75.

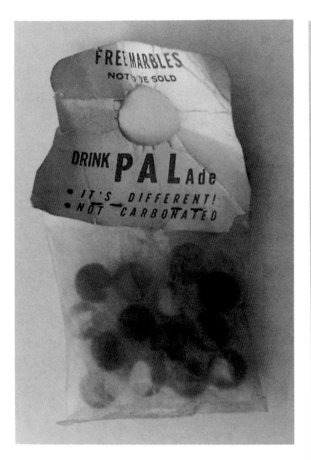

Advertising. Bottle Hanging Bag - PALade, Poly. $25-$50.

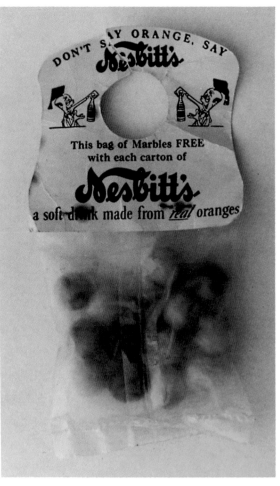

Advertising. Bottle Hanging Bag - Nesbitt's, Poly. $25-$50.

Game. Marbo Kangaroo Puzzler. (Contains Christensen Agate Swirls.) $200-$500

Game. Ten Pin Bowling. (Contains Heaton Agate Swirls.) $15-$30.

Other. Assorted Marble Pouches and Bags. (All old except first row, third bag) $5-$100.

Other. MAR-BO-GUN Marble Shooter. $15-$30 (on card), $5-$10 (off card). *Courtesy Block's Box.*

Other. Assorted Marble Pouches and Bags (New). $5-$10 each.

Other. Marbl-Matic Marble Carrier. $45-$90.

Section IV:
CONTEMPORARY MARBLES

Mark P. Block

CONTEMPORARY MARBLES

Since the first edition of *Marble Mania*®was published in 1997, collectible contemporary marbles have seen a continued and sustained growth. This growth is evident by viewing the multitude of styles and types of contemporary marbles, and experienced artists and craftsmen who create them.

A short ten years ago you would find it difficult to name more than a dozen or so well-known artists. Today, you can easily count dozens of artists working in both soft and hard glass, at the furnace or torch, or crafting hand painted and decorated china and polymer clay marbles.

Contemporary marbles are differentiated from other collectible marbles in a few ways. Primarily, these are works of art in glass or other media. The works are nearly always signed, and are crafted for display not play. Today's contemporary artists are designing some wonderfully beautiful marbles. These marbles may evoke the style of antique handmade swirls, onionskin or Joseph's Coat designs, or more recent machine-made marbles, like guineas, slag's and swirls. Additionally, the effect of the Studio Glass Movement propelled marble artists into the world of truly contemporary designs. Many are large display pieces that can be exhibited easily in curio cabinets, on desks or tables, whether singly or in groupings.

Contemporary marbles are most often classified into three distinct groups: rod- and cane-cut/hot glass, torchwork, and hand painted China. These three groups can be broken down further into subgroups. For example, rod- and cane-cut can include marbles made in the antique-style, such as swirls and paperweight-style, lobed core and murrini. Others that are comprised primarily of millefiori, and still others that are handcrafted sulphides and marbles crafted in the graal technique developed by Orrefors in the early-1990s.

Marbles crafted at the torch are done so using soft (moretti) or hard (borosilicate) glass. These marbles are typically one-off works with each piece being distinctively different from the next. Whether a simple swirl or complex murrini piece using one glass rod or many, embellished or vortex design, torchwork marbles have seen the greatest growth occur over the last ten to twelve years. The ability of bead artists, pipe makers and those who set up their own in-house studio have easy and ready access to the tools and furnaces necessary to craft torchwork marbles.

China marbles are crafted by the artist from clay, fired and decorated. There have been a growing number of artists working in polymer clay in recent years as well. The beautiful murrini canes being crafted from clay and worked into a marble have opened up a whole new area of contemporary collecting. This is also true of enamel painted marbles and collaborative pieces. Again, any of these marbles can be simple in design or extremely detailed in the final composition. At times you will even see cross-over work. Some artists will do both rod- and cane-cut and torchwork pieces. Others will use a combination of techniques, including polymer clay over mass produced marble bases.

Throughout this chapter you will see works done by various artists working in each of the areas of today's contemporary handmade marble. You'll see some old-time favorite artist's works and newer younger craftsmen as well. Hopefully, many of the names you'll recognize and other will strike your fancy and encourage adding their works to your collection as well.

Due to space limitations it is nearly impossible to illustrate the work of every artist and craftsmen working in the Contemporary Marble Movement today. Other well-known books on the subject will give you a much more detailed history of the Contemporary Marble Movement and the artists and works they craft.

The work of the contemporary marble artist today can be purchased at any one of a number of galleries, web sites, auctions, or from the artist directly.

Rod- and Cane-Cut: Hot Glass

Abstract. Multi-color ribbon glass pieces with clear core. Virginia Wilson Toccalino. 3 in., ca 2003. *Courtesy private collection* $150-300

Stardust Clambroth. Alternating bands of yellow and green over blue and copper dichroic glass. Geoffrey Beetem. 1-3/8 in., ca. 2001. *Courtesy private collection. $70-150*

Megaplanet. Single gather. Josh Simpson. Josh Simpson Contemporary Glass. 8 in., ca. 2004. *Courtesy of the artist.* $90-5,000

Double Angelfish. Paperweight-style aquarium scene. David Salazar. 1-3/4 in. ca. 1998. *Courtesy private collection. $150-350*

Banded Swirl. Six-panel multi-color beach ball design. Rolf and Genie Wald. 1-1/2 in., ca. 2000. *Courtesy private collection. $50-100*

Onionskin. Yellow murrini stars over blue base. David Salazar. 1-11/16 in., ca. 1999. *Courtesy private collection. $90-180*

Joseph's Coat. Alternating multi-color bands with reverse twist. Fritz Lauenstein. 1-5/8 in., ca. 2003. *Courtesy private collection. $40-80*

Flowers. Paperweight-style ruffled flora over aventurine glass ground. David Salazar. 2-1/8 in., ca. 2003. *Courtesy private collection. $150-300*

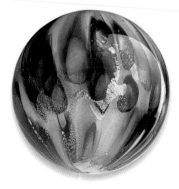

End-of-Day. Onionskin Cloud. White base with multi-color dichroic glass. Geoffrey Beetem. 2 in., ca. 2004. *Courtesy private collection. $80-160*

Abstract. Gaffer's Revenge. Multi-color various ribbon and latticinio cane in clear glass. James Alloway. 2-1/2 in., ca. 2008. *Courtesy of the artist. $150-300*

Paperweight-style murrini star canes with red and white canes in clear glass. Tony Parker. 1-5/8 in., ca. 1992. *Courtesy of Marble Collectors Society of America.* $50-100

Ribbon Swirl. Aventurine Ribbons. Multi-color aventurine glass bands in clear glass. Rolf and Genie Wald. 1-1/2 in., ca. 2007. *Courtesy of the artists.* $75-150

Paperweight-style murrini heart canes on blue and white over red. Kathy Young, Christopher Constantin. 1-1/2 in., ca. 1983-1989. *Courtesy of the Marble Collectors Society of America.* $50-100

Complex millefiori. Tube Garden. Packed murrini canes form complex millefiori design. Douglas Sweet. 2-1/4 in., ca. 2006. *Courtesy of private collection.* $125-250

Banded Swirl. Melon Balls. Translucent multi-color bands with aventurine in clear glass. Rolf and Genie Wald. 1-1/2 in., ca. 2007. *Courtesy of the artists.* $75-150

Complex Millefiori. Packed multi-color design murrini canes over black base form complex millefiori design. John Gentile. 2-3/4 in., ca. 2007. *Courtesy of private collection. $50-150*

Complex Millefiori. Packed multi-color design murrini canes, square cut and polished round. Gerry and Pat Colman. 1-3/8 in., ca. 2000. *Courtesy of private collection. $50-250*

Murrini Sphere. Checkerboard. Multi-color murrini canes create checkerboard pattern over black base. Jody Fine. 1-5/8 in., ca. 1986. *Courtesy of the Marble Collectors Society of America. $100-200*

Banded Swirl. Multi-color bands with lutz. Ryan Wilder. 2-1/4 in., ca. 2006. *Courtesy of the artist. $40-80*

Banded Swirl. Yellow and blue with dichroic glass fat ribbon swirl. Nina Paladino and Michael Hansen. 3-1/4 in., ca. 2008. *Courtesy of the artists. $50-100*

Banded Swirl. Red and blue with dichroic glass fat ribbon swirl. Nina Paladino and Michael Hansen. 3-1/4 in., ca. 2008. *Courtesy of the artists. $50-100*

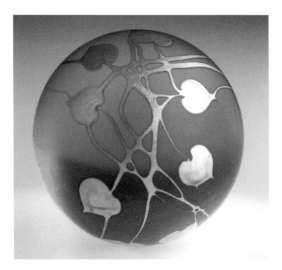

Hearts and Vines. Tiffany-style iridescent hearts and vines over matte red base. David P. Salazar. 1-3/4 in., ca. 2007. *Courtesy of private collection. $100-200*

Onionskin. Multi-color lobed onionskin. Brett Young and Larry Zengel. 2 in., ca. 2006. *Courtesy of the artists. $125-250*

Painted Scene. New England Spring. Enamel painted landscape scene encased in clear glass. Wendy Besett. 1-7/8 in., ca. 2002. *Courtesy of private collection. $250-500*

Scenic. Man in the Moon murrini cane with white murrini stars on a field of blue glass. David P. Salazar. 2-1/4 in., ca. 1998. *Courtesy of private collection. $250-500*

Filigrana. Multi-color twelve rod cane filigrana. Brett Young and Larry Zengel. 2-1/2 in., ca. 2006. *Courtesy of the artists. $175-350*

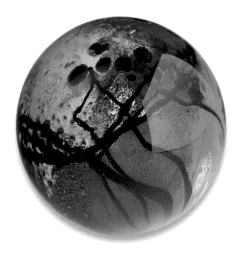

Abstract. Multi-color with dichroic glass. Shanti Devi. 1-5/8 in., ca. 1985. *Courtesy Marble Collectors Society of America. $75-150*

Cameo. Various cameo farm animals sandblasted on matte glass base. Harry and Wendy Besett. 1-1/2 in., ca. 2003. *Courtesy private collection. $50-100*

Banded. Melon-color crosshatch design with orange separating bands over black base. Kris Parke. 2-1/8 in., ca. 2005. *Courtesy of the artist. $125-250*

Floral. Paperweight-style yellow flower with air trap on red ground glass base. Joe Rice. 2 in., ca. 1993. *Courtesy of the Marble Collectors Society of America. $60-120*

Onionskin. Pulled lobe onionskin of red, white and blue with blizzard dichroic glass. Kris Parke. 2 in., ca. 2005. *Courtesy of the artist. $80-160*

Lobe Core. Rainbow Butterfly. Multi-color lobe core over white base. Eddie Seese. 2 in., ca. 2004. *Courtesy of the artist.* $75-150

Millefiori. 3-D Alien World. Multi-color assorted millefiori on blue base. Bobbie Seese. 2 in., ca. 2005. *Courtesy of the artist.* $50-100

Banded Swirl. Cosmos Tetrisphere. Multi-color with reverse twist over dichroic black base. Eddie Seese. 1-3/4 in., ca. 2005. *Courtesy of the artist.* $75-150

Single gather. Abraham Lincoln bust on multi-color ground glass base. Joe St. Clair. 2 in., ca. 1985. *Courtesy private collection.* $150-300

Sulphide. Single gather. Painted cow. Charles Gibson. 2-1/8 in., ca. 1997. *Courtesy private collection. $75-150*

Sulphide. Single gather. Painted duck. Jim Davis. 2-1/4 in., ca. 1999. *Courtesy private collection. $150-300*

Rainbow, 3D Back-Twist. Multi-color bands with reverse twist over black base glass. Drew Fritts. 1-7/8 in., ca. 2003. *Courtesy of the artist. $150-300*

End-of-Day. Onionskin. Four-panel stretched murrini with blue base and blizzard mica. Francis Coupal. 1-7/8 in., ca. 2003. *Courtesy private collection. $100-200*

End-of-Day. Onionskin. Multi-color bands with blizzard mica over white base. Drew Fritts. 1-7/8 in., ca. 2002. *Courtesy private collection. $125-250*

Torchwork: Moretti Glass and Borosilicate Glass

Murrini. Hummingbird and flora murrini with ribbon and rake pull. Jesse Taj. 1-1/2 in., ca. 2003. *Courtesy private collection. $100-200*

Vortex. Multi-color millefiori borosilicate cane with vortex design. Rajesh Kommineni. 2 in., ca. 2007. *Courtesy of the artist. $80-160*

Universe Marble. Fumed glass with inclusions. Gateson Recko. 3-1/4 in., ca. 2004. *Courtesy of private collection. $100-500*

Vortex. Filigrana borosilicate glass vortex. Rajesh Kommineni. 2 in., ca. 2006. *Courtesy of the artist. $80-160*

Flower Implosion. Orange with blue sparkle borosilicate flora. Joe Schlemmer. 2-1/8 in., ca. 2007. *Courtesy of the artist. $75-150*

Onionskin. Multi-color onionskin design over black base. Keith Baker. 1-3/16 in., ca. 2008. *Courtesy of the artist. $40-80*

Vortex. Borosilicate vortex with Gilson Opal. Chad Trent. 1-1/2 in., ca. 2008. *Courtesy of the artist. $60-120*

Flora with Ladybug. Purple floral with ladybug murrini. Brett Christian. 1-1/2 in., ca. 2007. *Courtesy of the artist. $75-150*

Sandblasted. White Rhinos. Color borosilicate sand carved white rhinos.
Kaj Beck. 1-5/8 in., ca. 2007. *Courtesy of the artist. $150-300*

Floral Garden. Multi-color flora over blue base. Cathy Richardson.
1-1/2 in., ca. 2003. *Courtesy of private collection. $75-150*

Snake. Paperweight-style green snake on ground glass base encased in clear
glass. Lewis and Jennifer Wilson. 2-3/8 in., ca. 2003. *Courtesy of private
collection.$200-400*

Metamorphic. Freeform banded sandblasted borosilicate glass.
Steve Sizelove. 2 in., ca. 2006. *Courtesy of the artist.* $75-150

Orchid. Phalaenopsis denevei, pale yellow orchid in soft glass.
Ken Schneidereit. 2-3/8 in., ca. 2006. *$225-350*

Dichroic Galaxy. Color glass center surrounded by black, borosilicate glass.
Steve Sizelove. 1-1/2 in., ca. 2004. *Courtesy of the artist.* $75-150

Orchid. Phalaenopsis amabilis, white with orange orchid in soft
glass. Ken Schneidereit. 2-3/8 in., ca. 2006. *Courtesy of the artist.*
$225-350

Graal. Handle with Care. Graal technique design over red glass. Jonathan Goldbert. 2-1/4 in., ca. 2005. *Courtesy of the artist.* *$75-150*

Abstract. Dichroic blue/green foil design with reverse rake pull design. Teri Conklin. 1-7/8 in., ca. 2002. *Courtesy private collection. $60-120*

Sea Florals. Multi-color sea flora in clear glass. Jerry Kelly. 1-1/4 in., ca. 2003. *Courtesy private collection. $60-120*

Vortex. Multi-color dichroic center, outer multi-color rake pull. Shell Neisler. 2-3/8 in., ca. 2003. *Courtesy private collection.* *$100-200*

Embellished. Multi-color rake pull with surface embellishments. Dinah Hulet. 1-1/2 in., ca. 1998. *Courtesy private collection. $150-300*

Scenic. River Salmon. Torchwork fish and underwater greens on sandy glass ground. Vacuum encased. Cathy Richardson. 3-1/8 in., ca. 2008. *Courtesy of the artist. $350-600*

Scenic. Frog with Cattails. Torchwork frog, cattails and lily ponds. Vacuum encased. Cathy Richardson. 3-1/4 in., ca. 2008. *Courtesy of the artist. $350-600*

Scenic. Sunset Prickly Pear Cactus. Torchwork cactus and stone sandy glass ground. Vacuum encased. Cathy Richardson. 3-1/4 in., ca. 2008. *Courtesy of the artist. $350-600*

Rake Pull. Scope '05. Multi-color rake pull design with reverse design and embellishment. Six and one facets. Daniel Benway. 3-1/4 in., ca. 2005. *Courtesy of the artist. $250-450*

Rake Pull. Cosmos Series. Multi-color rake pull. Brendan Blake. 1-1/2 in., ca. 2003. *Courtesy of the artist. $35-70*

Rake Pull. Lots of Mayhem. Multi-color rake pull design with reverse design and embellishment. Daniel Benway. 3-1/2 in., ca. 2004. *Courtesy of the artist. $200-400*

Rake Pull. Geode. Multi-color rake pull with windows. Brendan Blake. 1-1/4 in., ca. 2004. *Courtesy of the artist. $35-70*

Scenic. Poison Dart Frog on bed of Flowers. Paperweight-style effrete and schot ophthalmic glass. Flora and frog encasement. Lewis and Jennifer Wilson. 2-1/4 in., ca. 2005. *Courtesy of the artists. $200-400*

Flora. Two-sided paperweight-style flora. Beth Tomasello. 1-3/4 in., ca. 2005. *Courtesy of the artist. $150-300*

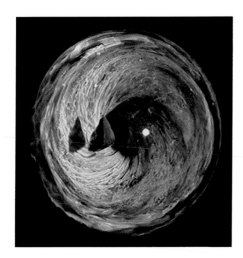

Vortex. Multi-color vortex with suspended opal chip. Lewis Wilson. 1-1/2 in., ca 2001. *Courtesy of the artist. $60-120*

Flora. Paperweight-style flora with multi-color reverse design. Beth Tomasello. 1-1/2 in., ca. 2005. *Courtesy of the artist. $100-200*

Eye. Green eye murrini with multi-color reverse design. Beth Tomasello. 1-1/4 in., ca. 2003. *Courtesy of the artist. $100-200*

Floral. Multi-petal orange flora in clear glass. John Kobuki. 1-3/8 in., ca. 2007. *Courtesy of the artist.* $75-150

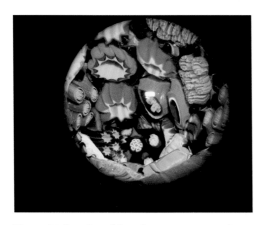

Vortex. Multi-color vortex with rake pull reverse. Kevin O'Grady. 1-1/2 in., ca. 2004. *Courtesy of the artist.* $150-300

Slag. Multi-color twisted bands. Richard Clark. 1-3/8 in., ca. 2007. *Courtesy of the artist.* $25-50

Slag. Multi-color twisted bands. Richard Clark. 1-3/8 in., ca. 2007. *Courtesy of the artist.* $25-50

Vortex. Multi-color tidal pool murrini vortex with rake pull reverse. Kevin O'Grady. 1-1/2 in., ca. 2006. *Courtesy of the artist.* $200-400

Guinea. Guinea-style multi-color encased in clear glass. Bruce Breslow. 1-1/4 in., ca. 2005. *Courtesy of the artist.* $40-80

Vortex. Multi-color fumed glass vortex with rake pull reverse. Kevin O'Grady. 1-7/8 in., ca. 2006. *Courtesy of the artist.* $250-450

Scenic. Underwater Carribbean scene. Murrini cane, dichroic glass. Cindy Hyer Morgan. 2 in., ca. 2004. *Courtesy of the artist. $150-300*

Reticello. Multi-color filigrana surrounding reticello design. Joshua Sable. 1-5/8 in., ca. 2002. *Courtesy of the artist. $80-160*

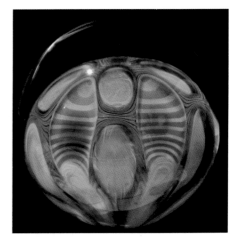

Abstract. Banded, pulled, dot Steppingstone with clear glass. Travis Weber. 1-5/8 in., ca. 2005. *Courtesy of the artist. $60-120*

Floral. Multi-color pulled dots with a rake pull design equator. Joshua Sable. 1-7/16 in., ca. 2002. *Courtesy of the artist. $100-200*

Floral. Orange crayon, autumn leaves cane, cherry red floral. Reverse dots and pinwheels. Nathan Miers. 1-3/4 in., ca. 2006. *Courtesy of the artist. $75-150*

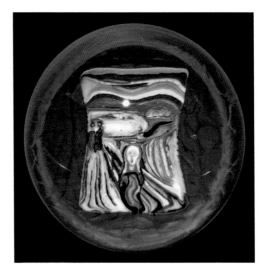

Gila Monster. Multiple millefiori canes surround central Gila monster murrini. Zachary Jorgenson. 1-1/2 in., ca., 2007. *Courtesy of the artist. $250-500*

The Scream. Complex millefiori cane interpretation of Evard Munch painting. Zachary Jorgenson. 1-1/2 in., ca., 2007. *Courtesy of the artist. $250-500*

Money Tree. Multiple checkerboard murrini canes creating patchwork quilt pattern. Zachary Jorgenson. 1-1/2 in., ca., 2007. *Courtesy of the artist. $175-300*

Marble Player. Central murrini cane marble player with surrounding bands and reverse rake pull. Dinah Hulet. 1-1/2 in., ca. 1998. *Courtesy private collection. $200-400*

Handpainted China,
Polymer and Other

Pinwheel with lines. Single gather, painted and glazed. Nadine Macdonald. 1-9/16 in., ca. 1999. *Courtesy private collection. $50-100*

Pinwheel with flora. Single gather, painted and glazed. Gregg Pessman. 1-3/8", ca. 2004. *Courtesy private collection. $50-100*

Etched lined. Single gather, painted and glazed. Nadine Macdonald. 1-1/8 in., ca. 2000. *Courtesy private collection. $25-50*

Pinwheel. Single gather, painted, crazed and glazed. Tom Thornburgh. 1-3/16". ca. 2002. *Courtesy private collection. $40-80*

Cape Cod Fern Garden. Single gather, painted flora on black base. Unglazed. Nadine Macdonald. 2 in., ca. 1999. *Courtesy private collection. $75-150*

Tiffany-style flora. Single gather, stained glass design, painted and glazed. Nadine Macdonald. 2-1/4 in., ca. 2003. *Courtesy private collection. $75-150*

Geometric checkerboard. Single gather, multi-color checkerboard pattern, painted and glazed. Gregg Pessman. 2-1/8 in., ca. 2003. *Courtesy private collection. $75-150*

Pigs in the Cornfield. Single gather, scenic pig design, painted and glazed. Gregg Pessman. 1-1/4 in., ca. 2002. *Courtesy private collection. $50-100*

Bennington-style. Single gather, mottled colors on white base, painted and glazed. Robert Brown. 1-3/4 in., ca. 1989. *Courtesy private collection. $40-80*

Dancing Pigs. Single gather, pinwheel with scenic pig design, painted and glazed. Gregg Pessman. 1-3/8 in., ca. 2002. *Courtesy private collection. $50-80*

Clown. Single gather, scenic clown, painted and glazed. Tom Thornburgh. 1-1/2 in., ca. 2000. *Courtesy private collection.* $45-90

Poinsettia. Single gather flora design, painted and glazed. Tom Thornburgh. 1-3/4 in., ca. 1997. *Courtesy private collection.* $50-100

MCSA Logo. Single gather, scenic Marble Collectors Society of America log and marbles, painted and glazed. Gregg Pessman. 1-3/8 in., ca. 2002. *Courtesy Marble Collectors Society of America.* $75-150

Angel. Single gather, angel with murrini clay cane, painted and glazed. Coralee Smith. 1-3/8 in., ca. 2001. *Courtesy private collection. $75-150*

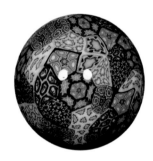

Crazy Quilt. Multi-color millefiori style patterned after antique crazy quilt. Polymer clay baked. Carl Fisher. 1-1/4 in., ca. 2007. *Courtesy of the artist. $45-90*

Rural Scene. Single gather, scenic pinwheel design, painted and unglazed. Nadine Macdonald. 1-3/8 in., ca. 1999. *Courtesy private collection. $50-100*

Millefiori. Multi-color paperweight-style patterned after antique weight. Polymer clay baked. Carl Fisher. 3/4 in., ca. 2007. *Courtesy of the artist. $50-100*

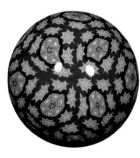

Flora and insects. Polymer baked murrini and millefiori flora and insect slices over clear glass.
Pat Wilson. 1-1/8 in.-1-1/4 in., ca. 2008. *Courtesy of the artist.$25-50*

Section V:

GAMES AND TOYS

Scott McBride and Stanley A. Block

INTRODUCTION

Marble games can be divided into categories such as Playground Games, Tournaments, and Board Games. A listing of games and toys is included.

A secondary collectible was created by the various tournaments, such as the medals, pinbacks, badges, and trophies used and presented. A national tournament has been held since 1922, and is currently held in Wildwood, New Jersey, each June.

PLAYING MARBLES AND MARBLE GAMES

The game of marbles is one of the oldest and most widespread games believed to exist. Archaeologists have discovered small round spheres at ancient sites in Egypt, India, Greece, and the United States. The various games using marbles are played in almost every part of the world. From Wildwood, New Jersey, to Beijing, China, to Shankhouse, Northumberland in England, children of all ages can be seen taking careful aim at marbles. Almost any store that carries a line of toys will certainly have packages of marbles just waiting for a boy or girl to buy them and challenge their friends to a game.

Abacys	Conqueror		Long Taw	Peirilia (Cyprus)	Shooting Gallery (wood w/3
Aggravation	Corner the Cow	Handlers	Losing yur Marbles	Persian	dogs)
Akro Solitary Checkers	Corner the Market	Handy Candy	Lost Marble Puzzle	Pick Off	Shooting the Ring
Alleus	Corona	Handy Dandy		Picking the plum	Single Hole
Amish Marble Puzzle	Croquet	Hit	Mancala	Picking Plums	Skelly
Arch Board		Hit the Span	Marble Arch	Pigs in Clover	Skip Ball
Attention	Da Bawh Ji	Hit the Spot	Marble Billiards	Pigeon Hole	Sliding Marbles
	Dead Ducks	Holi Lkes	Marble Bingo	Piggy	Snops and Spns
Bagatelle	Dicies	Holy Bang	Marble Bocce	Pinball with Marbles	Solitaire
Basketelle	Die Shot	Ho-Go	Marble Golf	Boomerang	Space Marbles (Magnetic)
Big Ring	Dobblers	Hundreds	Marble Jacks	Disneyland	Span (England)
Big Tennessee	Double Ring Taw		Marble Maze	Mickey Mouse	Spangy
Birds in the Bamboo	Dowsie	Increase Pound	Marble Mill	Pop-A-Puppet	Spanning (Spanners)
"Bizzy Andy" Triphammer	Dropsies	Indian (Injun)	Marble Minder	Roll Bowl	Spinners
Black Snake	Duck in a Hole	Immie	Marble Shoot Game	Pig or Pot	Stadium Checkers
Block	Duck Shoot	International Airport	Meg in a Hole	Poison	Stand Up Marbles
Bombers			Meg on a String	Poison Circle	Stay Alive
Boss (England)	Eggs in the bush	Jorrah (Africa)	Milkie	Poison Hole	Sticker
Boss Out	English Ring Taw		Moon Ring	Poison Pot	String of Beads
Bounce About		Keller Eng (Indonesia)	Moshie	Poison Ring	Square Dancing
Bounce Eye	Fat	Ker Plunk	Mosaic	Pot II	Square Ring
Bowls	Followings	Killer		Potsies	
Boxies	Follow On	King Duck	Nine Holes	Potty	Three Holes
Bridge Board	Football	Knickelie	Nine Marbles	Prince Henry	Three and Your own
Brownie Auto Race	Forts	Knucks	Nine Pins	Puggy	Tic-Tac-Toe
Bull Ring	Fortifications	Knuckle Box	Newark Killer	Purees	Tin Hen (Lays Eggs)
Bullseye	Fox and Geese		Nucks	Pyramid	Toodlembuck
Bullseye Marble Shooter		Labyrinth			Torpedo
Bun Hole	Gade (Brazil)	Lagging	Obstacles	Rebound	Trap Door
	General Grant	Lag Out	Odd or Even	Ringer (Ringo)	Trunks
Capture	German Balls	Lampie	Off the Wall	Ring Taw	Twenty One
Castles	Giggle Wiggle	Last Clams	Old Bowler	Rockies	
Chasies	Golf	Line Up		Rollem Through	Wa-Hoo
Cherry Pit	Goli Panjang	Linie	Packman	Rolley Hole	Wall
Chinese Checkers	Ground hog	Little Pig	Pails of Fun	Rolly Polly	War
Circle	Gude	Little Ring	Pallino di Vetro (Italy)		
Commies	Gutterie	Long Ring	Pattersou	Shoot-A-Loop	

GAMES AND TOYS

Marbles appear in commercially produced games as playing pieces. Walk through nearly any toy store, and games like "Hungry Hippos," "Stuff Yer Face," "Ker Plunk," and "Marblehead" can be seen. According to a Marble King release, the most popular game using marbles today is "Chinko-Checko-Marblo." Chinese Checkers is the more common name for the game that uses sixty marbles and is played by both young and old. It is a game that seems truly to cross generational lines. There have been many other games that use marbles, however, like many consumer goods, their availability on the market was short-lived, and can now be found primarily at flea markets and tag sales.

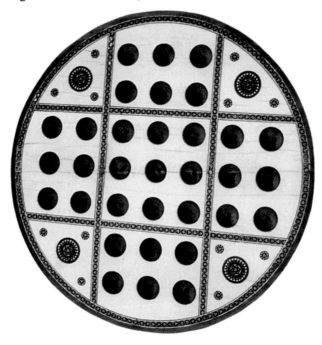

Decorated Solitaire Game Board. Too Rare to Value. *Collection of Elliot Pincus.*

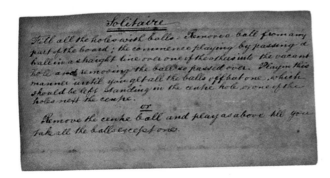

Instructions. Too Rare to Value. *Collection of Elliot Pincus.*

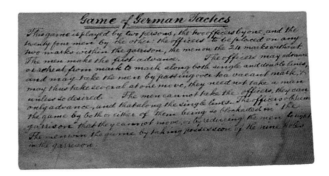

Reverse of Instructions. Too Rare to Value. *Collection of Elliot Pincus.*

Solitaire Game. $300-$500. *Collection of Elliot Pincus.*

Game of Pigs. $75-$150. *Courtesy of Block's Box.*

Solitaire Game. $75-$100. *Courtesy of Block's Box.*

Whirl It Game. $75-$150. *Courtesy of Block's Box.*

Game of Laripino. $75-$150. *Collection of Elliot Pincus.*

Tivoli Game. $200-$400.
Courtesy of Block's Box.

Tivoli Game. $200-
$400. *Courtesy of
Block's Box.*

Game of Skill Ball. $50-$100.
Courtesy of Block's Box.

American Marble
Game - Earlier Form
of Skill Ball. $75-$150.
*Courtesy of Block's
Box.*

Scarlet O'Hara. $50-$100.
Courtesy of Block's Box.

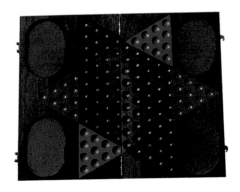

Game of Circus Tivoli.
$200-$400. *Collection of
Elliot Pincus.*

Folding Wood Chinese
Checkers Board. $40-$75.
Courtesy of Block's Box.

Game of Circus Tivoli.
$200-$400. *Collection
of Elliot Pincus.*

Hopalong Cassidy Chinese Checkers Game. $50-$100.
Courtesy of Block's Box.

Ball Mosaic. $50-$100.
Courtesy of Block's Box.

Marble Puzzle Blocks. $200-
$400. *Courtesy of Block's Box.*

Meteor Game. $50-
$100. *Courtesy of
Block's Box.*

Cloth Counting Book. $50-$100. *Collection of
Elliot Pincus.*

Building and Designing Set.
$50-$100. *Courtesy of
Block's Box.*

Cloth Counting
Book Page Eight.
$50-$100. *Collection
of Elliot Pincus.*

BOYS NATIONAL CHAMPIONS

Following are the tournament winners and runners-up since the inception of the National Marbles Tournament in 1922. Also included are the offical rules of play.

1922
Winner: "Bud" McQuade
Baltimore, MD
Runner-Up: (Ms) Babe Ruth
Newark, NJ

1923
Winner: Harland McCoy
Columbia, OH

1924
Winner: George Lenox
Baltimore, MD
Runner-Up: Tom Wright
Springfield, MA

1925
Winner: Harold Robbins
Springfield, MA
Runner-Up: Tom Riley
Owensboro, KY

1926
Winner: William Harper
Beview, KY
Runner-Up: Danny Gore
Springfield, MA

1927
Winner: Joe Medvicovich
Pittsburgh, PA
Runner-Up: Teddy Walag
Springfield, MA

1928
Winner: Alfred Huey
Akron, OH
Runner-Up: Con Cartelli
New Britain, CT

1929
Winner: Charles Albany
Philadelphia, PA
Runner-Up: Mike Batche
Akron, OH

1930
Winner: James Lee
Columbus, OH
Runner-Up: Floyd Walker
Decatur, IL

1931
Winner: John Jeffries
Greenville, KY
Runner-Up: Harley Corum
Louisville, KY

1932
Winner: Harley Corum
Louisville, KY

Runner-Up: E. T. Weisberger
South, NJ

1933
Winner: Aaron Butash
Throop, PA
Runner-Up: Bill Mathews
Chattanooga, TN

1934
Winner: Cliff Seaver
Springfield, MA
Runner-Up: Sidney Deitz
Baton Rouge, LA

1935
Winner: Henry Altyn
Throop, PA
Runner-Up: Bill Truedell
Springfield, MA

1936
Winner: Leonard Tyner
Chicago, IL
Runner-Up: Andrew Tanana
Throop, PA

1937
Winner: Bill Koss
Canton, OH
Runner-Up: Andrew Tanana
Throop, PA

1938
Winner: Frank Santo
Throop, PA
Runner-Up: Joe Baltrusaitis
Scranton, PA

1939
Winner: Harry DeBoard
Landenburg, PA

1940
Winner: James Music
Huntington, WV
Runner-Up: Charles Mott
Huntington, WV

1941
Winner: Gerald Robinson
Scranton, PA
Runner-Up: George Wolfe
Throop, PA

1942
Winner: Charles Mott
Huntington, WV
Runner-Up: Jack Kean
Canton, OH

1943
Winner: Dick Ryabik
Pittsburgh, PA

1944
No Tournament (World War II)

1945
No Tournament (World War II)

1946
Winner: Benjamin Ryabik
Pittsburgh, PA

1947
Winner: Don Sklar
Pittsburgh, PA

1948
Winner: Herman Truman
Beloit, WI
Runner-Up: Stan Morris
Huntington, WV

1949
Winner: George Wentz
Huntington, WV
Runner-Up: Bob Brady
Greensboro, NC

1950
Winner: Bob Retzlaff
Montgomery, AL
Runner-Up: Fred Cunningham
Huntington, WV

1951
Winner: Shirley Allen
Beckley, WV
Runner-Up: Bob Kupchak
Scranton, PA

1952
Winner: Russ Gwaltney
Salem, VA
Runner-Up: Jim Lilly
Beckley, WV

1953
Winner: Jerry Roy
Huntington, WV
Runner-Up: John Gaetano
Throop, PA

1954
Winner: Bob Hickman
Huntington, WV
Runner-Up: Frank Bartroney
Wilkes Barre, PA

1955
Winner: Ray Jones
Pittsburgh, PA
Runner-Up: Dick Hickman
Huntington, WV

1956
Winner: Fred Brown
Beckley WV
Runner-Up: Dennis Kyle
Richwood, WV

1957
Winner: Stan Herold
Summersville, WV

Runner-Up: Dennis Kyle
Richwood, WV

1958
Winner: Dennis Kyle
Richwood, WV
Runner-Up: Dick Hickman
Huntington, WV

1959
Winner: Mat Wysocki
Wilkes Barre, PA
Runner-Up: Charles Duffy
Summersville, WV

1960
Winner: Tom Meade
Yonkers, NY
Runner-Up: Dick Kimsal
Wilkes Barre, PA

1961
Winner: Ace Millen
Yonkers, NY
Runner-Up: Tom Senita
Yonkers, NY

1962
Winner: Mark O'Mahoney
Pittsburgh, PA
Runner-Up: Tom Senita
Yonkers, NY

1963
Winner: Jim Donohue
Springfield, MA
Runner-Up: John Riccardi
Yonkers, NY

1964
Winner: Clarence Bower
Mullens, WV
Runner-Up: Lou Harris
Cumberland, MD

1965
Winner: Garry Malcolm
Elkhart, IN
Runner-Up: Gregory Fulk
Greensboro, NC

1966
Winner: Melvin Garland
Pittsburgh, PA
Runner-Up: Ken Stasiak
Pittsburgh, PA

1967
Winner: Barry Blum
York, PA
Runner-Up: Rudy Raymond
Reading, PA

1968
Winner: Rudy Raymond
Reading, PA
Runner-Up: Glenn Sigmon
Wharton, WV

1969
Winner: Glenn Sigmon
Wharton, WV
Runner-Up: Ray Morgano
Pittsburgh, PA

1970
Winner: Ray Morgano
Pittsburgh, PA
Runner-Up: Larry Kokos
Pittsburgh, PA

1971
Winner: Rick Mawhinney
Cumberland, MD
Runner-Up: Matt Joyce
Pittsburgh, PA

1972
Winner: Ray Jarre11
Whitesville, WV
Runner-Up: Matt Joyce
Pittsburgh, PA

1973
Winner: Doug Hager
Whitesville, WV
Runner-Up: Don Vergalitta
Yonkers, NY

1974
Winner: Larry Kokos
Pittsburgh, PA
Runner-Up: Jeff Rice
Cumberland, MD

1975
Winner: Richard Usner
Allegheny Co., PA
Runner-Up: Jeff Rice
Cumberland, MD

1976
Winner: Jeff Rice
Cumberland, MD
Runner-Up: Walt Morgano
Allegheny, Co., PA

1977
Winner: Walt Morgano
Allegheny Co., PA
Runner-Up: Charles Holstein
Naoma, NY

1978
Winner: Dean Feinauer
Reading, PA
Runner-Up: Mark Zupsic
Allegheny Co., PA

1979
Winner: Danny Stamm
Reading, PA
Runner-Up: Chuck Bosiljevac
Allegheny Co., PA

BOYS NATIONAL CHAMPIONS

1980
Winner: Sandy Nesmith
Arnett, WV
Runner-Up: Antoine Hayes
Robeson Co., NC

1981
Winner: Jeff Kimmell
Cumberland, MD
Runner-Up: Byron Ford
Robinson Co., NC

1982
Winner: Mike Moore
Cumberland, MD
Runner-Up: Kerry Acord
Arnett, WV

1983
Winner: Kerry Acord
Arnett, WV
Runner-Up: Carmel Burnside
Mt. View, WV

1984
Winner: Greg Yakich
Allegheny Co., PA
Runner-Up: Tim Suhr
Northbridge, OH

1985
Winner: Jon Jamison
Reading, PA
Runner-Up: Toby Carlile
Cumberland, MD

1986
Winner: Giang Duong
Upper Darby, PA
Runner-Up: Shawn Jackson
Drexel Hill, PA

1987
Winner: Chad Reber
Berks Co., PA
Runner-Up: Shawn Jackson
Drexel Hill, PA

1988
Winner: Dan Strohecker
Reading, PA
Runner-Up: Brett Shaffer
Cumberland, MD

1989
Winner: Nicky Piatek
Allegheny Co., PA
Runner-Up: Brett Shaffer
Cumberland, MD

1990
Winner: Carl Whitacre
Ridgeley, WV
Runner-Up: Mickey Lantz
Ridgeley, WV

1991
Winner: Brian Shollenberger
Reading, PA
Runner-Up: Justin Krause
Allegheny Co., PA

1992
Winner: Wesley Thompson
Standing Stone Park, TN
Runner-Up: Nathan Thompson
Thompkinsville, KY

1993
Winner: David McGee
Allegheny Co., PA
Runner-Up: Brett Johnson
Walkersville, MD

1994
Winner: Buong Duong
Upper Darby, PA
Runner-Up: Nathan Thompson
Monroe County, PA

1995
Winner: Jason Williams
Sports Festival, WV
Runner-Up: Nathan Thompson
Monroe County, KY

1996
Winner: Nathan Thompson
Monroe County, KY
Runner-Up: Jeff Staus
Cumberland, MD

1997
Winner: Michael Thomas
Upper Darby, PA
Runner-Up: Danny LaGambo
Allegheny, PA

1998
Winner: Ben Nelson, 14
Frederick, MD
Runner-Up:

1999
Winner: Doug Watson, 14
Greencastle, PA

Runner-Up: Andrew Martinez, 13
Grand Junction, CO

2000
Winner: Andrew Martinez, 14
Grand Junction, CO
Runner-Up: Ralph Pillon, 14
Doddridge County, WV

2001
Winner: Tim Ratliff
Runner-Up: Jon Leatherman

2002
Winner: John Hurse
Hagerstown, MD
Runner-Up:

2003
Winner: Jeremy Hulse
Washington City, MD
Runner-Up:

2004
Winner: Aaron Nees
Mesa County, CO

Runner-Up:

2005
Winner: Jamie Miller, 11
Pittsburgh, PA
Runner-Up: Raymond McFarrano, 13
Lansdowne, PA

2006
Winner: Keith Moss
Allegheny County, PA
Runner-Up:

2007
Winner: Nick Anderson
Mesa County, CO
Runner-Up:

2008
Winner: Jeff Leffakis, 14
Lawrenceville, PA
Runner-Up:

2009
Winner: Ricky Brode
Cumberland, MD
Runner-Up: Christopher Cooproder
Lansdowne, PA

2010
Winner:
Runner-Up:

GIRLS NATIONAL CHAMPIONS

1948
Winner: Jean Smedley
Philadelphia, PA
Runner-Up: Carol Birchfield
Canton, OH

1949
No Record Available

1950
Winner: Kay Allen
Greensboro, NC

1951
Winner: Ida Hopkins
Cleveland, OH

1952
Winner: Dorothy Hobbs
Augusta, GA
Runner-Up: Jeanette McClincey
Lakewood, OH

1953
Winner: Arlene Riddette
Yonkers, NY
Runner-Up: Sonia Azam
Greensboro, NC

1954
Winner: Wanita Kuchar
Philadelphia, PA
Runner-Up: Martha Anderson
Augusta, GA

1955
Winner: Karen Olson
Niles, OH
Runner-Up: Marianne Cody
Yonkers, NY

1956
Winner: Lynette Watkins
Philadelphia, PA
Runner-Up: Vietta Ward
Dayton, OH

1957
Winner: Lois Fusco
Yonkers, NY
Runner-Up: Margaret Leonard
Niles, OH

1958
Winner: Jeanette Merlino
Yonkers, NY
Runner-Up: Sandra Wallace
Cleveland, OH

1959
Winner: Sandra Stefanchik
Yonkers, NY
Runner-Up: Margaret Leonard
Niles, OH

1960
Winner: Christine Zamoiski
Yonkers, NY
Runner-Up: Carol Mabry
Philadelphia, PA

1961
Winner: Anita Danyluk
Niles, OH

Runner-Up: Carol Mabry
Philadelphia, PA

1962
Winner: Peggy Mullen
Pittsburgh, PA
Runner-Up: Patsy Coon
Philadelphia, PA

1963
Winner: Patsy Coon
Philadelphia, PA
Runner-Up: Charlene Mills
Baltimore, MD

1964
Winner: Claudia Davis
Yonkers, NY
Runner-Up: Patricia Lowry
Pembroke, NC n

1965
Winner: Jacqueline Izaj
Pittsburgh, PA
Runner-Up: Marcella Elliott
Wilmington, DE

1966
Winner: Marcella Elliott
Wilmington, DE
Runner-Up: Connie Barton
Pembroke, NC

1967
Winner: Pat Yurkovich
Pittsburgh, PA
Runner-Up: Kathy Lochlear
Pembroke, NC

1968
Winner: Debbie Webb
Yonkers, NY
Runner-Up: Ivelisse Morales
Philadelphia, PA

1969
Winner: Maureen Regan
Pittsburgh, PA
Runner-Up: Eleanor Rice
Cumberland, MD

1970
Winner: Karen Yurkovich
Pittsburgh, PA
Runner-Up: Eleanor Rice
Cumberland, MD

1971
Winner: Cheryl Elliott
Wilmington, DE
Runner-Up: Eileen Kearney
Alexandria, VA

1972
Winner: Kathy Pazkowski
Pittsburgh, PA
Runner-Up: Dianna Hodges
Radford, VA

1973
Winner: Debra Stanley
Reading, PA
Runner-Up: Gloria, Webb
Yonkers, NY

1974
Winner: Susan Regan
Pittsburgh, PA
Runner-Up: Debbie Linaberg
Cumberland, MD

1975
Winner: Sharon Woolworth
Reading, PA
Runner-Up: Jerrilyn Keene
Baltimore, MD

1976
Winner: Judy Bosiljevac
Allegheny County, PA
Runner-Up: Jerrilyn Keene
Baltimore, MD

1977
Winner: Dianne Kopicki
Reading, PA
Runner-Up: Jerrilyn Keene
Baltimore, MD

1978
Winner: Diane Bertosh
Allegheny County, PA
Runner-Up: Denise Ricci
Allegheny County, PA

1979
Winner: Kris Alfiero
Reading, PA
Runner-Up: Joelle Guiles
Reading, PA

1980
Winner: Brenda Schwartz
Pottstown, PA
Runner-Up: Jina Bosiljevac
Allegheny County, PA

1981
Winner: Joelle Guiles
Reading, PA
Runner-Up: Lisa Stamm
Reading, PA

1982
Winner: Lisa Stamm
Reading, PA
Runner-Up: Mary Regan
Pittsburgh, PA

1983
Winner: Patricia Kimmell
Cumberland, MD
Runner-Up: Nicole Stamm
Reading, PA

1984
Winner: Nicole Stamm
Reading, PA
Runner-Up: Shellie Jamison
Reading, PA

1985
Winner: Amy Thompson
Cumberland, MD
Runner-Up: Shellie Jamison
Reading, PA

1986
Winner: Darlene Schwartz
Berks County, PA
Runner-Up: Shellie Jamison
Reading, PA

1987
Winner: Lori Dickel
Ridgeley, WV
Runner-Up: Shellie Jamison
Reading, PA

1988
Winner: Shannon Capasso
Allegheny County, PA
Runner-Up: Donna Rothenberger
Reading, PA

1989
Winner: Donna Rothenberber
Reading, PA
Runner-Up: Dawn Lancaster
Cumberland, MD

1990
Winner: Alison Reber
Oley, PA
Runner-Up: Ann McHugh
Lansdowne, PA

1991
Winner: Dawn Lancaster
Cumberland, MD
Runner-Up: Jaime Travis
Oley, PA

1992
Winner: Trish Tressler
Fredrick County, MD
Runner-Up: Ann McHugh
Upper Darby, PA

1993
Winner: Amanda Burns
Clay County, TN
Runner-Up: Kim Shuttleworth
Allegheny County, PA

1994
Winner: Kim Shuttleworth
Allegheny County, PA
Runner-Up: Stephanie Zlokas
Allegheny County, PA

1995
Winner: Stephanie Zlokas
Allegheny County, PA
Runner-Up: Heidi Stevenson
Reading, PA

1996
Winner: Molly Reecer
Clay County, TN
Runner-Up: Megan Pilarcik
Frederick County, MD

1997
Winner: Megan Winkelman
Frederick City, MD
Runner-Up: Megan Pilarcik
Frederick County, MD

1998
Winner: Emily Martin, 12
Frederick, MD
Runner-Up:

1999
Winner: Kathy Stehlik, 11
Perry Hall, MD
Runner-Up: Larin Miller, 11
Allegheny County, PA

2000
Winner: Larin Miller, 11
Allegheny County, PA
Runner-Up: Stephanie Taylor, 13
Cumberland, MD

2001
Winner: Kristy Vanderzee
Runner-Up: Krissie ONeill

2002
Winner:
Runner-Up:

2003
Winner: Jennifer Pinciotti
Frederick County, MD
Runner-Up:

2004
Winner: Carli Miller
Alleghenny County, PA
Runner-Up:

2005
Winner: Amy Nees, 13
Palisade, CO
Runner-Up: Heidi Griswold, 13
Perry Hall, MD

2006
Winner: Melissa Ashwood
Gunnison, CO
Runner-Up:

2007
Winner: Alexandra Bauer
Allegheny County, PA
Runner-Up:

2008
Winner: Amber Ricci, 12
Shaler, PA
Runner-Up:

2009
Winner: Whitney Lapic
Berks County, PA
Runner-Up: Penelope Bauer
Allegheny County, PA

2010
Winner:
Runner-Up:

OFFICIAL RULES OF PLAY

TOURNAMENT GAMES

The game played in the National Marbles Tournaments is called "Ringer." The National Marbles Championship Tournament has been held annually since 1922 in Wildwood, New Jersey, on the third weekend of June. The best marbles players, as determined by local and state contests, meet to compete for the title of National Champion. Here are the rules from the 1931 Marble Tournament, as published in an Akro Agate flyer. They are essentially unchanged in play today.

Description:

RINGER is played in a ring ten (10) feet in diameter, with thirteen (13) marbles arranged in the center in a cross. The object is to shoot these marbles out of the ring, the player shooting the largest number of marbles out of the ring in any game being the winner of that game. No less than two and no more than six may play in one game in RINGER, except in national championship matches two only play. All tournament plays is for fair, and marbles must be returned to owners after each game.

Equipment

The playing surface shall be a smooth level area of ground, hard clay, or other suitable substance. The Ring is inscribed upon this area, 10 feet in diameter, and all play is within this ring. (Note: The outline of this ring shall not be so deep or so wide as to check the roll of a marble). With the center of the Ring as a point of intersection, mark two lines at right angles to each other to form a cross, which shall be a guide for placing the playing marbles. Place one marble at the center and three on each of the four branches of the cross, each marble three inches away from the next one. The Lag Line is a straight line drawn tangent to the Ring and touching it at one point. The Pitch Line is a straight line drawn tangent to the Ring, directly opposite and parallel to the Lag Line. All marbles in any one playing ring must be of uniform size. The standard size shall be five-eighths inch in diameter. Slight variation may be allowed by the referee for

manufacturing fault. Shooters shall be round and made of any substance except steel or any other metal, and shall not be less than one-half inch nor more than six-eighths inch in diameter as determined by the referee.

Plan of Play

The lag is the first operation in RINGER. To lag, the players stand toeing the Pitch Line, or knuckling down upon it, and toss or shoot their shooters to the Lag Line across the ring. The player whose shooter comes nearest the Lag Line, on either side, wins the lag. Players must lag before each game. The player who wins the lag shoots first, and the others follow in order as their shooters were next nearest the Lag Line. The same shooter that is used in the lag must be used in the game following the lag. On all shots, except the lag, a player shall knuckle down so that at least one knuckle is in contact with the ground, and he shall maintain this position until the shooter has left his hand. Knuckling down is permitted, but not required in lagging. Starting the game, each player in turn shall knuckle down just outside the Ring Line, at any point he chooses, and shoot into the ring to knock one or more marbles out of the ring, or to hit or knock out of the ring the shooter of an opposing player, or players, if any remain inside the ring. If a player knocks one or more marbles out of the ring, or hits the shooter of an opponent, or knocks an opponent's shooter out of the ring he continues to shoot provided his own shooter stays in the ring. He ceases to shoot after his first miss, and then is credited with the marbles he has scored. If, after a miss, a player's shooter remains inside the ring, he must leave it there and his opponents are permitted to shoot at it. If the shooter rolls outside the ring, he picks it up and on his next shot is permitted to take roundsters and shoot from any point on the Ring Line.

Playing Regulations

Marbles knocked out of the Ring shall be picked up by the player who knocks them out. If his shooter stays in the ring he continues to shoot. If not, he stops, and his opponent starts shooting. Whenever a marble or shooter comes to rest on the Ring Line, if its center is outside the Ring, or exactly on the Ring Line, it shall be considered out of the Ring; if its center is inside the Ring, it shall be considered inside the Ring. A player hitting an opponent's shooter inside the Ring, but not knocking it out, shall pick up any marble he chooses, and if his own shooter stays in the ring shall continue to shoot. However, he shall not hit the same opponent's shooter again until after he hits another shooter, or knocks a marble out of the Ring, or he comes around to his next turn to shoot. A player knocking an opponent's shooter out of the Ring and stopping his own shooter in the ring shall be entitled to all the marbles won by the opponent, and the opponent whose shooter has been knocked out of the Ring is out of the game, "killed." If the opponent who was knocked out of the Ring has no marbles, the player who knocked him out shall not be entitled to pick up a marble for the shot. If a shooter knocks out two or more marbles, or hits an opponent's shooter and a marble, or hits two opponent's shooters, or completes any other combination play, he shall be entitled to all points scored on the shot. When a shooter slips from a player's hand, if the player calls "slips" and the referee is convinced that it is a slip, and if the shooter did not travel more than 10 inches the referee may order "no play" and permit the player to shoot again. The referee's decision is final. The game shall end when the last marble is shot out.

Scoring

For each marble knocked out by a player, he shall be credited with the score of ONE. For each time a player hits the shooter of an opponent, and does not knock it out of the ring, he shall be credited with a score of ONE. For each time a player knocks an opponent's shooter out of the ring, he shall be credited with all the marbles, previously scored by the hit opponent. The player having credited to him the largest number of marbles at the completion of the game shall be the winner of that game. In games where more than two players are engaged, if two or more players lead with the same score, those in the tie shall play a new game to break the tie. A player refusing to continue a game, once it is started, shall be disqualified, and if only two players are engaged, the game shall be forfeited to the offended player. The score of a forfeited game shall be 13-0.

Officials

The officials shall be a referee and a scorer, if a scorer is available, otherwise the referee shall also keep score.

The referee shall have complete charge of the play. He shall interpret these rules and have power to make decisions on any points not specifically covered by these rules. He shall have authority to disqualify any player for unsportsmanlike conduct. He shall have authority to order from the playing field or its vicinity the coach or other representative of any player, who conducts himself improperly. The scorer shall keep a record of the game, marking score of each player, shot by shot, and at the termination of each game shall notify the referee of the score, and the referee shall announce the winner. The scorer shall assist the referee in enforcing the rule against coaching, and call to the attention of the referee any infraction of the rules.

Penalties

A player shall NOT:

Lift his hand until the shooter has left his hand. This violation is known as "histing". Move his hand forward until the shooter has left his hand. This violation is known as "hunching". Smooth or otherwise rearrange the ground, or remove any obstacles. He may request the referee to clear obstructions. Penalty (for any one of these three violations): If any marbles were knocked out or dislocated on the shot, they shall be restored to their place, and the player shall lose his shot.

Change shooters during the course of the game. He may choose a new shooter on lag, provided he uses that shooter in the subsequent game. Penalty: The player shall be disqualified from the game.

Communicate in any way with his coach during the course of the game. Penalty: Forfeiture of all marbles he has knocked out of the ring, said marbles to be returned to the game and placed on the cross.

A coach shall not give instructions to either his own or any other player engaged in the game. Penalty: Coach shall be ordered from the playing field, if, after be warned once, he continues this violation.

Players must not walk through the marble ring. Penalty: After a player has been warned for violation, the referee MAY require the forfeiture of one marble, on a second offense, said marble to be returned to the ring and placed on the cross.

Stereopticon Card - Marble Players. $25-$50. *Collection of Hansel deSousa.*

Stereopticon Card - Marble Players. $25-$50. *Collection of Hansel deSousa.*

Stereopticon Card - Marble Players. $25-$50. *Collection of Hansel deSousa.*

Reverse of V-27. $25-$50. *Collection of Hansel deSousa.*

Stereopticon Card - Marble Players. $25-$50. *Courtesy of Block's Box.*

Trade Cards - Chocolates (France). $40-$75. *Collection of Hansel deSousa.*

Trade Cards - Cigarettes. $40-$75. *Collection of Hansel deSousa.*

Reverse of V-29. $40-$75. *Collection of Hansel deSousa.*

Reverse of V-31. $40-$75. *Collection of Hansel deSousa.*

Trade Card - England. $40-$75. *Collection of Hansel deSousa.*

Madam Porter's Cough Balsam. Card. $40-$75. *Collection of Hansel deSousa.*

Reverse of V-33. $40-$75. *Collection of Hansel deSousa.*

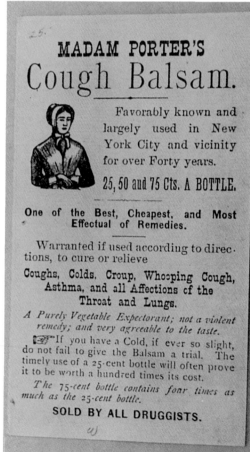

Reverse of Madam Porter's Cough Balsam. $40-$75. *Collection of Hansel deSousa.*

Van Horten Chocolates Card. $40-$75. *Collection of Hansel deSousa.*

Century of Progress - Master Marble House. $60-$100. *Collection of Hansel deSousa.*

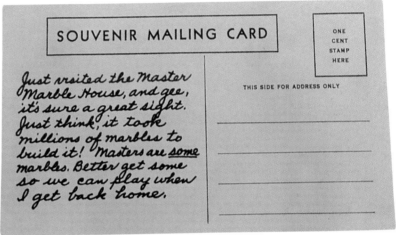

Reverse of Century of Progress - Master Marble House. $60-$100. *Collection of Hansel deSousa.*

French Marble Players. $40-$75. *Collection of Hansel deSousa.*

Reverse of French Marble Players. $40-$75. *Collection of Hansel deSousa.*

The Marble Tournament, Ocean City, N. J.

Ocean City, New Jersey, Marble
Tournament (Front). $60-$100.
Collection of Hansel deSousa.

Ocean City, N.J. Marble
Tournament (Back). $60-$100.
Collection of Hansel deSousa.

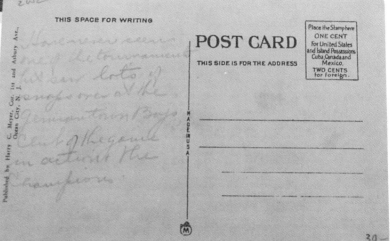

No Fudging Post Card.
$40-$75. *Collection of
Hansel deSousa.*

Game of Ringer Post Card. $40-
$75. *Collection of Hansel deSousa.*

An Anxious Moment Post Card. $40-$75. *Collection of Hansel deSousa.*

French Marble Trade Card - 1885 (Front). $40-$75. *Collection of Hansel deSousa.*

French Marble Trade Card - 1885 (Back). $40-$75. *Collection of Hansel deSousa.*

An Exciting Moment Post Card (Back). $40-$75. *Collection of Hansel deSousa.*

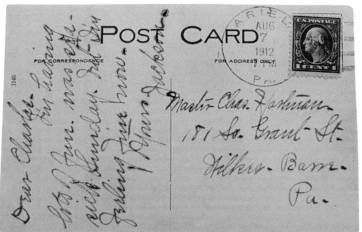

Boy Holding Carpet
Bowl (Back). $20-$40.
(Dated August 7, 1912.)
*Collection of Hansel
deSousa.*

Boy Holding Carpet Bowl (Front).
$20-$40. *Collection of Hansel deSousa.*

When We Were Kids. $40-$75. *Collection of Hansel deSousa.*

Trade Card (Front). $40-$75. *Collection of Hansel deSousa.*

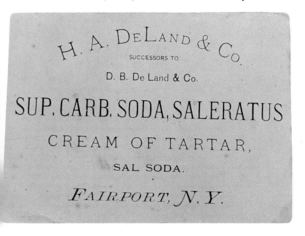

Trade Card (Back).
$40-$75. *Collection of
Hansel deSousa.*

French Post Card. $40-$75. *Collection of Hansel deSousa.*

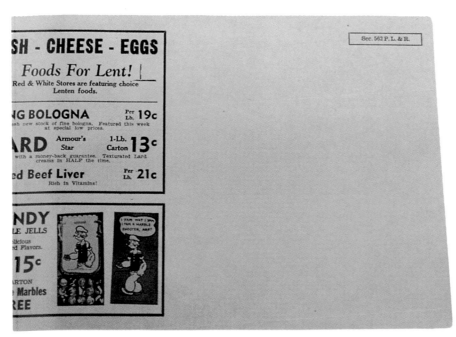

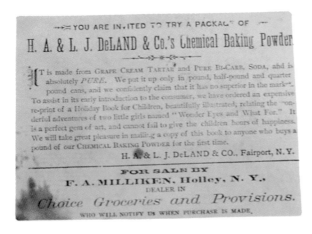

Top left: Ad Card (Front). (March 18-19, 1938.) $40-$75. *Collection of Hansel deSousa.*

Top right: Ad Card (Back). $40-$75. *Collection of Hansel deSousa.*

Center left (one): Trade Card (Front). $40-$75. *Collection of Hansel deSousa.*

Center left (two): Trade Card (Back). $40-$75. *Collection of Hansel deSousa.*

Bottom left: Marble Playing Stamps. $25-$50. *Courtesy of Block's Box.*

Center right: Post Card. $40-$75. *Collection of Hansel deSousa.*

Group Shot - Tournament Medals. $4,500-$8,000; $150-$500 each.

Tournament Medals (3). $200-$400 each.

Tournament Medal. $200-$400.

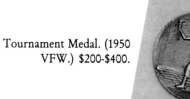

Tournament Medal. (1950 VFW.) $200-$400.

Back of above. $200-$400.

Officials - Tournament Medal. $300-$500.

Tournament Medal (1931). $200-$400. *Collection of Hansel deSousa.*

Tournament Medal (1931). $300-$500. *Collection of Hansel deSousa.*

Tournament Medal (1934). $200-$400. *Collection of Hansel deSousa.*

Tournament Medal. $200-$400. *Collection of Hansel deSousa.*

Tournament Medal (1934). $300-$500.

Tournament Badge & Ribbon. Michigan (1940). $150-$300.

Tournament Badge & Ribbon. Oregon (1939). $150-$300. *Courtesy of Block's Box.*

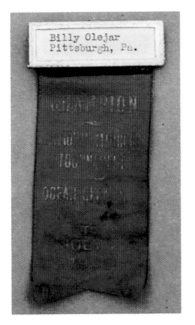

Tournament Badge & Ribbon. National. $100-$300.

Official Press Medal (1933). $300-$500. *Collection of Hansel deSousa.*

Knuckle Down Pin
Back. $50-$100.
*Collection of Hansel
deSousa.*

Players Pin Back
(1940). $50-$100.
*Collection of Hansel
deSousa.*

Lancaster, Pennsylvania, Pin Back (1924).
$50-$100. *Collection
of Hansel deSousa.*

Marble Shooter Pin
Back (1928). $50-
$100. *Collection of
Hansel deSousa.*

"13 in 1" Club. $50-
$100. *Collection of
Hansel deSousa.*

Harrisburg, Pennsylvania, Pin Back
(1929). $50-$100. *Collection of Hansel
deSousa.*

Harrisburg, Pennsylvania, Pin Back
(1931). $50-$100. *Collection of Hansel
deSousa.*

Detroit Free Press
Pin Back. $50-$100.
*Collection of Hansel
deSousa.*

Star Times Pin Back. $50-$100.
Collection of Hansel deSousa.

Harrisburg, Pennsylvania,
Pin Back (1931). $50-
$100. *Collection of Hansel
deSousa.*

Chicago Journal Pin Back.
$50-$100. *Collection of
Hansel deSousa.*

Atlantic City
Shooter Bronze.
Too Rare to Value.
*Collection of Hansel
deSousa.*

The Marble Shooter. Too Rare to Value. *Collection of Scott McBride.*

Sterling Tournament
Trophy Cup. $400-$700.
Courtesy of Block's Box.

Seventh National Marble Bronze (1929). Too
Rare to Value. *Collection of Scott McBride.*

Marble Statue. Too Rare to Value.
Collection of Scott McBride.

Tournament
Trophy. $200-
$400. *Courtesy of
Block's Box.*

OTHER USES

by Scott McBride and Stanley A. Block

INTRODUCTION

This section lists many of the uses of marbles other than as toys. It shows that marbles have many practical uses and have also been used to create unique collections.

COMMERCIAL AND INDUSTRIAL USES OF MARBLES

Commercial and industrial uses of marbles are related to the process of mass production. As the availability of marbles increased, so did their practical uses. Marbles used commercially are usually produced to exact specifications. These marbles really are not collectible because of the huge quantities that have been manufactured, but it is interesting to know how marbles are used in industrial and commercial applications.

- Along with a solution of emery and oil, marbles are used by lithographers to polish copper plates to the desired finish for use in the printing process.
- Filters for some oils and acids also use glass marbles. When it is necessary for gasses to pass through these liquids, marbles can be used in special condensing units where they allow the gasses to pass slowly through the condenser unit without the marbles becoming corroded by the acids.
- If you have ever used an aerosol spray can, you may have encountered a personal use of marbles. A small marble is placed inside each can before it is filled and sealed. When you shake the can before use the marble stirs up and mixes the contents. Without the marble, much of the can's contents might be wasted.
- The rising concern about oil conservation has added another use for marbles. Glass marbles are pumped through old oil wells to clean them and increase their productivity.
- Glass spheres are now used in the process of spinning glass thread. Research has shown that a glass sphere heated to a certain temperature will allow a fine glass thread to be taken from its outside surface. Eventually, the entire sphere can be made into one long glass thread.
- Marbles can be found in some valves and have been used as bottle stoppers. The marble forms the seal when the valve is closed.
- Marbles can be found in paper mills where they are used in the paper feeding process. The marbles keep the paper flowing smoothly. In earlier mills, stone spheres were used for this purpose, but glass spheres have proven more durable.
- Marbles have found a use in fish hatcheries. Small piles of marbles are placed around the bottom of the spawning pool. Male fish believe them to be eggs and the result is increased spawning activities.
- If your spouse snores, it has been proven that a marble may stop the snoring. Just sew a single marble into a small pocket in the middle of the back of their pajamas, right between the shoulder blades. Since most snoring happens while a person is asleep on their back, this appears to prevent snoring.
- Marbles can also be used to keep milk, wine, or any other drink that spoils fresher longer. Once the container has been opened, it is the air inside the container that causes spoilage. You can use "wine keepers" to keep the beverage fresh. Just drop the marbles into the container and the level of the liquid will rise, forcing the air out of the container, preventing spoilage. As more is drunk, just add more "wine keepers."
- Some small businesses and florists use marbles in vases in place of a flower frog. The marbles can hold either real or artificial flowers in place and they add an attractive touch to the arrangements. Products using marbles are commercially available that do the same function. Two such products are "The Arranger" and the "Crystal Ball Flower Ring."
- Marbles have been used as ball bearings and rollers. Many stories have been told concerning the use of marbles to move heavy objects around warehouses and boxcars before small lift trucks were used. A handful of marbles have also been thrown into mausoleum crypts, enabling the casket to roll easier.

New uses for glass spheres or marbles will be found for both industrial and commercial applications as companies continue to grow and change.

CRAFT MARBLES

A once-popular use for marbles was in craft work. Marbles, along with other common materials, can still be made into many beautiful, useful, and unusual items to decorate the home. The book *Magic with Marbles* illustrates many of the items that can be created with marbles. Marbles used for craft projects are usually the most common marbles. Many craft marbles are different from collectible marbles because they have been "crystallized." This is done by heating the marbles in an oven or frying pan for about thirty minutes, then dropping the marbles into cold water. Internal fractures result, thus giving the marbles a crystallized appearance. The marbles are also known as "fried" or "cracked" marbles. The marbles themselves are not collectible but some of the things made with them can add an interesting dimension to any marble display.

Marbles have been used on lamps, decorative grapes, "critters and creatures," pyramids, and kaleidoscopes. Marbles are also used as eyes for dolls and stuffed animals. The most famous use of marbles for eyes is the "Flying Horses" carousel. The carousel, listed in the National Historic Register, is located in Oak Bluffs, Massa-chusetts, and the hand-carved horses have yellow sulphides for eyes.

Around some homes, marbles can be found embedded in cement sidewalks and bird baths, in planters, and at the bottom of aquariums. They can also be found acting as knobs on wooden boxes, as glass parts for miniature lanterns, part of a clock's mechanism, and as a toy ball in a small Santa Claus' bag. Anywhere that small round objects are added to decorations, marbles can be used.

Another craft use of marbles is for costume jewelry. Necklaces, bracelets, rings, watch fobs, hat pins, tie clips, and key chains have all been designed with marbles as their major adornment. Marbles have also been used as buttons and cuff links, and glass marbles and stone spheres have been part of the lapidarian and jeweler's art for many years. Some examples of this use of marbles are exceptional in the quality of workmanship and in the quality of the marbles used. If you look around at flea markets and craft shows, you'll be surprised how many different items use marbles.

COLLECTIBLE USES OF MARBLES

A lot of thought has been given to the question of what makes a marble collectible useful. Uniqueness seems to be a large part of what to look for in an item that uses marbles. The more unusual the use of marbles, the more desirable it is to have such an item in your collection. Some collectors also consider the rarity of the marble itself. An item that uses a highly collectible marble is more desirable than an identical item with a more common marble. Another criterion would be if the marble item is collected by people whose collections are not marble specific. Being desirable by more than one type of collector increases the value of any item. Some uses of marbles are very difficult to locate specific information on. Sometimes the marbles used aren't even recognized as being marbles. Every marble collector must decide for themselves what type of collectibles they want in their collection and what limitations they are going to use in choosing examples they will display. What follows is a listing of many different collectible items that include marbles in their construction. As mentioned earlier, it is the marbles themselves that make these items sought after by collectors.

LAMP KNOBS

Many lamp knobs have used marbles as accents for shape and color. The round shape is pleasing to the eye, and colors can be found to match almost any base or shade. There are several different styles of lamp knobs using marbles. The one that appears older has the marble glued into a metal, funnel-shaped base. Another style has four metal prongs shaped like petals holding the marble in place. A third style uses thin metal prongs to hold the marble secure. The marble in the last two styles is loose and can be turned or even removed from the base. The sizes of marble used varies, but the original marble is almost always machine made. The major difference in the different lamp knobs is the base and how it holds the marble in place.

CLAW FEET

Piano stools and tables have been created with beautiful claw feet clutching glass spheres. The size of these "marbles" seems to range from about 1-1/2 inches on piano stools and smaller tables to 3 inches on larger, heavier tables. Often the claw feet are accents that are hardly noticed when compared to the fine workmanship of the furniture they are attached to. Usually the claws hold clear glass spheres, but occasionally the "marbles" are colored glass. Sometimes sulphides or other more collectible marbles have been used to replace damaged spheres.

TOWEL HOLDERS

How much would you give for a product that could promise "no more unsightly nails or disfigured walls, increased service life of your linens, and no torn towels and no towels on the floor"? All of these claims can be found on the Erickson Towel Holder box. A marble was the trick that made all of this possible. By inserting the towel with an upward movement, a ball would drop down and hold it firmly in place. The towel was removed by a slight pull upward and to the side.

These towel holders were metal, with a base color of white or black. Some used a clay marble and others used a machine made one. Often, advertising items like the Erickson Towel holder are highly prized by advertising collectors, or collectors of local memorabilia, as well as marble collectors.

Similar to the Erickson Towel Holders are towel or note holders made of metal, or even wood, which use the same principle. There are several different designs using a marble as the pincher to hold things. Little is known about most of them because they exhibit no manufacturer's markings or patent numbers.

BROOM HOLDERS

Another household device that used a marble and gravity to do a job was a broom holder. To make use of this device, you would put the broom handle in the holder with an upward motion, as it dropped down, the marble would pinch the handle and it would hold the broom neatly and out of the way until needed.

One type of broom holder is similar in construction to the Erickson Towel Holder. It was apparently offered as a premium from businesses to their customers. This holder used a blue Bennington marble as the pincher and is marked "The Augustine Co., Sept. 17, 1917."

The second type of broom holder was much smaller and made out of cast metal. It is likely the oldest of the two broom holders. The only marking it exhibits is on the back, "Pat. Jan. 10, 1893". It is a gold color that appears to have been added at a later date. Originally, it was probably bare metal. No history of the manufacturer or its distribution is currently known.

CODD SODA BOTTLES

Codd Soda Bottles or Marble Stopper Bottles trace their history back to 1870. Hiram Codd, operator of a mineral works in England, designed a bottle for aerated beverages with "an annular groove in the neck to hold a cork or rubber washer." The bottle would be filled upside down and the washer would form seating for an internal glass ball stopper. The bottle would be stored for a short period of time upside down, then the pressure inside would hold the marble tightly sealed. To open the bottle, you only had to dislodge the marble by pushing down on it with a finger or narrow rod.

Several problems developed with the original design of the marble stopper bottle. When the marble was dislodged, it would fall to the bottom, sometimes breaking the bottle. Also, when pouring soda from the bottle, the marble would float back into the neck of the bottle, resealing it. The first problem was solved in 1871 by adding a pinch near the base of the bottle's neck, preventing the marble from falling to the bottom. The resealing problem was corrected in 1872 when the specifications for the bottle were changed to include a pair of lugs in the neck, designed to hold the marble out of the way when the contents were being poured.

The Codd Soda Bottle was patented in the United States in 1873, and the marbles used in them have been identified as dark green, light blue, dark blue, amber, and clear glass. The marbles appear to be handmade with many showing evidence of a pontil mark. It is possible that some of the clear, handmade marbles already in your collection might be all that is left of a Codd Soda Bottle.

COFFEE POT

For years it has been suggested that putting a marble in the bottom of a coffee or tea pot keeps mineral deposits from settling to the bottom of the pot. It has been claimed that the marble helps by making the water softer. As a rule, marbles found in the bottom of coffee pots are not highly collectible, but what if you found a coffee pot with a marble as a functional part of the pot? That is exactly what the Silver Company of Brooklyn, New York, did with their Marion Harland Tea & Coffee Pot. The marble wasn't in the bottom of the pot, but enclosed in the spout. In a turn-of-the-century Marion advertisement, the marble is mentioned as a "valve." When the pot is upright, the marble fits snugly at the base of the spout, probably to prevent the coffee or tea from boiling out of the spout as it was being brewed. When the pot is held in a pouring position, the marble rolls up the spout to a point where two small, metal bands hold it, allowing the coffee or tea to be poured out. These pots used a brown Bennington marble.

WHISTLES

An unusual use of a collectible marble can be found in metal whistles. These marbles serve only decorative functions in the whistle. They have been seen with two marbles, one marble, and no marbles. They roll inside three metal rods about 3-1/4 inches long, attached to round, hollow metal caps at both ends. The whistling sound is made by blowing through the hole in either end of the whistle.

RAZOR BLADE SHARPENERS

Knives and razor edges can be kept keen with a small, simple device known as a razor blade sharpener. Wire frames hold two glass marbles together, with the knife or razor drawn between the marbles. They form a near-perfect angle for smoothing the edge of the blade and removing rough spots. The marbles used are common machine made marbles, usually clearies. They all turn freely in the wire frame, being held in place by the tension of the frame. Style differences in the forms of the wire handles suggest that different manufacturers produced the razor blade sharpeners. Markings on one handle has an identification reading "Pat. Pend."

A different type of razor blade sharpener has a wooden handle attached to a metal frame that holds two steel balls in place. The inside base of the metal frame says "Others pend. Patd. 9-25-23." On the exterior of the frame, the name ACE is enclosed in a diamond shape. This razor blade sharpener was advertised in magazines during the 1920s as the "Ace Rotary Strop."

BALLOT BOXES

History indicates marbles have long been a part of the democratic process in America. Ballot boxes with marbles are used by many fraternal organizations and clubs throughout the country. Every ballot box comes with two colors of marbles: white and black, which are used to cast the votes. The white marble represents a "yes" vote and the black marble a "no" vote. The ballot box itself is usually divided into two compartments. At least one side of the ballot box had a lid that could be kept closed during balloting to ensure secrecy. At the start of voting, both colors of marbles are placed in the open compartment. The voter chooses the color of marble that corresponds to the manner in which he or she wishes to vote, placing that marble in the closed compartment. After all votes have been cast, they are tallied by counting the number of white "yes" marbles and black "no" marbles. If the issue was defeated, it was termed to be "black balled."

Most ballot boxes are simple wooden boxes, usually less than 12 inches long. There is often a handle on the box that allows it to be extended to voters sitting in rows of chairs. New ballot boxes use glass marbles, and older ones use glazed crockery marbles.

There are some ballot boxes which are unique. One ballot box had a hollow log mounted on a wood box. The log was standing on its end and the top had a felt basket in the end of the log, holding the black and white marbles. On the side of the log was a knot hole that was the spot where the marbles were cast. The marbles would fall through the log into the base which had a drawer in it to collect them.

CASH REGISTERS

Before the invention of mechanical adding machines and cash registers, marbles could be used by shop owners to keep track of their daily receipts. Originally, the Waddell Company of Greenfield, Ohio, and later Sun Manufacturing Company, produced the Simplex Cash Register. The register was constructed of wood and had two drawers. One drawer held the money and the second drawer held marbles that were dropped in the drawer to correspond with the amount of each individual sale. At the end of the day, the shop keeper needed only to "count his marbles" to get the day's total. Some cash registers used steel balls and others used clay marbles. These cash registers are rare and can usually only be found in the collections of avid cash register collectors.

WHISKEY BOTTLE STOPPERS

"The new Automatic bottle stopper" has two things in common, whiskey and marbles. Made by the Ball Stopper Company of Racine, Wisconsin, the Bottle Stopper was a pouring spout that fit snugly into the mouth of a bottle of liquor. The stopper was made with silver-plated brass and had a cork around the base to form a seal with the bottle. The marble sat on top of the spout in a small cage-like structure. When pouring, the marble would roll away from the spout allowing the liquor to flow freely. When the bottle was placed upright, the marble rolled over the spout, closing it. As the box the stoppers came in states, they were "an ornament to any bar, and a great timesaver." The markings on the stoppers say "Ball Stopper Co., Racine Wis." and "Pat."

FISHER JEWEL TRAYS

The Fisher Jewel Tray dates from the 1930s, and was made by the Fisher Manufacturing Company. It has a brass covering holding the "jewels" in place. These "jewels" were solid colored marbles, all of the same color. The Fisher Jewel Trays came in two sizes, the smaller size using twelve 5/8 inch marbles, the larger trays used fourteen 1 inch marbles. Some of these trays have a smooth finish, others an embossed texture, and some were identified with the symbol of the 1933 Chicago World's Fair.

Markings on the backs vary, with some saying "Fisher Jewel Tray", others saying "Fisher Master Jewel Tray", and a few include "Pat. 20945 29-Des. 99857." Others show "Pat. 99857." They were also manufactured with no markings on them, and were used primarily as ashtrays.

ROAD SIGNS AND REFLECTORS

Before the invention of reflector tape and glow-in-the-dark paints, round glass spheres were used to make signs more visible and warn drivers of slow moving traffic ahead. Reflectors of different styles and designs were manufactured for this specific road safety purpose.

CURRENCY MARBLES

For an object to serve as money, it must be easily recognizable and be readily accepted in trade. Many items throughout history have served as currency, examples include feathers, stones, tobacco leaves, and tea. In some primitive cultures, marbles have even served as currency. Round spheres with specific patterns or painted designs have been used as a medium of exchange. Marbles of clay, stone, and glass have also served that purpose.

Small Box - Agate Marbles for Feet (Top View). $300-$500.

HEAT RETAINERS

Marbles have also been used to keep people warm. In the earlier days of the horse and buggy, rows of China marbles were sewn into lap robes as heat retainers. Before going out on a cold night, you would wrap your buggy robe around the potbelly stove to get it warmed. The China marbles would hold the heat longer than a robe alone could and your ride would be more comfortable, as long as you weren't sitting on the marbles, because you would stay warmer longer.

Wax Seal with Banded Agate Marble. $200-$400. *Collection of Jeff Yale.*

Group Shot - Agate Marble Items. $700-$1,200. *Collection of Scott McBride.*

Wax Seal with Banded Agate Marble. $200-$400.

Wax Seal with Banded Agate Marble. $200-$400.

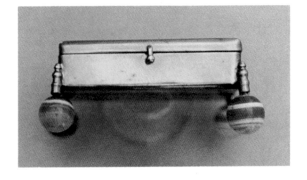

Small Box - Agate Marbles for Feet. $300-$500.

Wax Seal with Gray Banded Agate Marble. $200-$400.

Wax Seal with Banded Agate Marble. $200-$400.

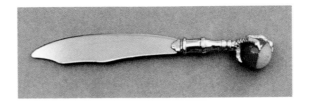

Letter Opener with Banded Agate Marble. $200-$400. *Collection of Jeff Yale.*

Book Mark with Banded Agate Marble. $200-$400. *Collection of Jeff Yale.*

Button Hook with Banded Agate Marble. $100-$200. *Collection of Jeff Yale.*

Hatpin with Banded Agate Marble. $50-$100. *Collection of Jeff Yale.*

Letter Opener with Dyed Banded Agate Marble. $200-$400.

Letter Opener with Dyed Agate Marble. $300-$500. *Collection of Jeff Yale.*

Shoe Horn with Banded Agate Marble. $200-$400. *Collection of Jeff Yale.*

Salamander Holding Large Banded Agate Marble. $200-$400. *Collection of Jeff Yale.*

Group of Razor Sharpeners. $75-$100.
Collection of Lefty Bingman.

Metal Marble Shooter. $50-$100. *Collection of
Hansel deSousa.*

Metal Marble Shooter. Counter
Display. $200-$400. *Courtesy of
Block's Box.*

Marble Cannon. $100-$200. *Courtesy of
Block's Box.*

Razor Sharpener Instructions (Front).
$25-$50. *Collection of Hansel deSousa.*

Sterling Ring with Half a Marble.
$100-$200. *Collection of Scott McBride.*

Razor Sharpener Instructions (Back). $25-$50. *Collection of
Hansel deSousa.*

Wonder
Crystal-Sharpener
FOR
RAZORS AND BLADES
Lasts a Lifetime
Money Back Guarantee
With This Device Blades Can Be
Used Over and Over Again

DIRECTIONS

For best results moisten sharpener :-
Hold sharpener level, draw blade straight
down between crystal balls very lightly.
Do this several times until smooth and sharp.

Manufactured by

**Wonder Specialities
Co.**
18 West 65th St.
New York City

PRICE 25 CENTS

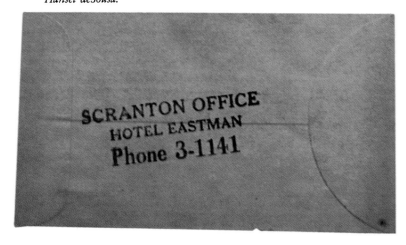

Sterling Bracelet with Half a Marble. $200-$400. *Collection of Scott McBride.*

Marble Jewel Trays. $100-$200. *Courtesy of Block's Box.*

Marble Playing Cards. $200-$400. *Courtesy of Block's Box.*

Marble Ash Tray. $50-$100.

Marble Playing Cards. $200-$400. *Collection of Hansel deSousa.*

Marble Tray with Clock Insert (Front). Too Rare to Value. *Collection of Emily Mullen.*

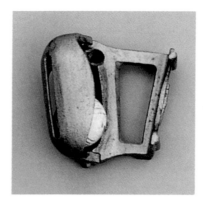

Broom Holder - China Marble. $100-$200. *Collection of Anonymous.*

Marble Tray with Clock Insert (Back). Too Rare to Value. *Collection of Emily Mullen.*

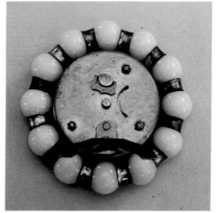

Pewter Bottle Pourer with Marble. $100-$200.

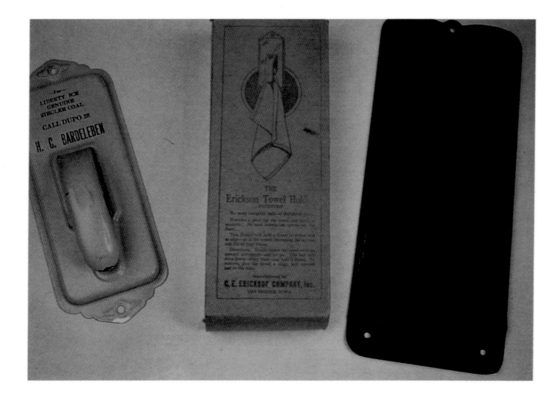

Erickson Towel Holder - China Marble. $200-$400. *Collection of Scott McBride.*

Codd Bottles with Marbles. $60-$100. *Collection of Scott McBride.*

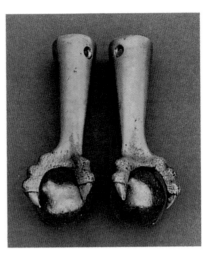

Claw Feet with Sulphides. $200-$400. *Collection of Trudy and Andy Christian.*

Hollow China with Bell Inside. Too Rare to Value. *Collection of Hansel deSousa.*

Reflections Using Marbles. $60-$100. *Collection of Scott McBride.*

Early Tile with Marble Players. $100-$200. *Courtesy of Block's Box.*

Cup with Marble Game. $50-$100. *Collection of Elliot Pincus.*

Chocolate Covered Marbles Box. $200-$400. *Courtesy of Block's Box.*

Norman Rockwell Marble Players Plate. $25-$50. *Courtesy of Block's Box.*

Chocolate Covered Marbles Box (Side View). $200-$400. *Courtesy of Block's Box.*

Chocolates Ad with Marble Players. $100-$200. *Courtesy of Block's Box.*

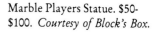

Norman Rockwell Marble Players Statue. $50-$100. *Courtesy of Block's Box.*

Marble Players Statue. $50-$100. *Courtesy of Block's Box.*

Original Blank
Christiansen Agate
Co. Invoice. $25-$50.
Courtesy of Block's Box.

Ink Well with Marble Stopper. $50-$100. *Courtesy of
Block's Box.*

Ballot Box. $100-$200. *Courtesy of Block's Box.*

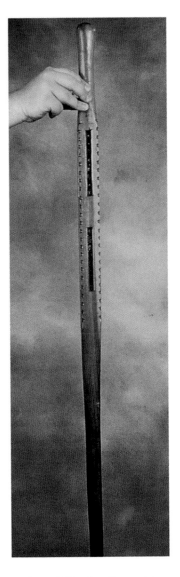

Wrought Iron Fireplace Poker -
Sulphide in Handle. Too Rare to
Value. *Collection of Scott McBride.*

Marble Counter Display.
$200-$400. *Courtesy of
Block's Box.*

Carved Wooden Cane with
Marbles Inside. Too Rare to
Value. *Collection of Scott
McBride.*

MISCELLANEOUS USES OF MARBLES

As you begin to be aware of items which use marbles to add to your collection, you may come across some that weren't mentioned here. These items likely were not made in large quantities, were made by individual craftsmen, or were made to meet a limited demand. There are many fine examples of these types of items: a wire meat fork with marbles woven in the wire handle, a wooden cane with marbles placed inside the cane, or forged fireplace tools made with a sulphide marble in the handle; all highly collectible items that use a marble for decoration. Other examples include a wooden shelf with mica marbles set in the wood, a cake plate that has sulphide marbles for feet, and silverware with a decorative claw tightly gripping a small marble.

Over the years many ideas have been explored by advertising agencies to get their messages to the customer. Radio, television, magazines, and newspapers are some of the media where advertising can be noticed everyday. Items such as milk cartons and postage stamps are commonly considered to be prime candidates for this kind of advertising. But what about marbles? Both the marbles and the packages they come in have been used to reach consumers.

What better idea than using the bags which marbles come in to deliver your message? Soft drinks could attract young consumers and their parents by hanging a bag of marbles on every carton like Pepsi®, Coke®, and Tower Root Beer® have done in the past. Children would ask their parents to buy the Red Goose® or Weather Bird Shoes® because their friends had a box of marbles they received with their new shoes. Tony's Cities Service of Lombard, Illinois, gave packages of marbles to their customers to remind them that "It Pleases Us to Please You." Mr. Peanut® and Mayrose Ready-to-Eat Ham® not only advertised their products but did a public service by reminding children to "Play the Game, Be Fair—Don't Cheat and Don't Play on the Street." Peltier Glass Company made packages of marbles that gave suggestions on how to use the marbles, and a West Virginian politician once gave packages of marbles with his name on them to people who attended his campaign rallies.

Even the marbles themselves have been used to carry messages. The Cotes Bakery advertised their products on a comic-strip marble. It has also been rumored that a dairy and President Herbert Hoover had the same idea for keeping their name prominent for people to see. Today, new advertisers have their logos and names printed on marbles. The new advertising marbles are larger than the older marbles and the printing is done on the outside surface of the marble and can be scratched off easily. Some companies utilizing this type of advertising include some of America's major corporations including Coca Cola and General Motors.

Another "message marble" is the Golden Rule Marble. This marble is made from synthetic materials and has a brass band around the equator of the marble. The words "do unto others as you would have them do unto you," are printed on the band.

The final "marble with a message" isn't selling anything. It is a prognosticator. "Fortune Telling Marbles" can answer any question or they can even predict your luck. Just ask the marble a question and roll it. If an even number is on top, the answer to your question is "yes" and if an odd number comes up, the answer is "no." The Fortune Telling Marble can also give specific answers to questions about love, marriage, finance, the home, luck, and surprise. All you need is the Fortune Telling Marble and the booklet with the answers that correspond to the numbers on the marble.

Marbles have had a varied past, a diverse present and an expanding future. When looking at a marble, collectors see much more than round glass. To collectors, marbles can be a poor man's jewels or a rich man's treasures.

LIMITED EDITION WALKING STICK

A limited edition of twelve walking sticks each containing one marble from each of fourteen West Virginia marble companies plus a 2: diameter Sam Hogue contemporary marble of Guinea style in gold and blue colors with ? to feature the West Virginia state colors. The walking sticks were crafted by John Ash from West Virginia black walnut wood.

The fourteen West Virginia marble companies represented are:

Akron Agate Company
Alley Agate Company
Bogard Company
Cairn Novelty Company
Champion Agate Company
Davis Marble Company
Heaton Agate Company
Jackson Marble Company
Marble King
Master Marble
Mid-Atlantic of West Virginia
Play Marble Company
Ravenswood Novelty ??
Vitro Agate Company

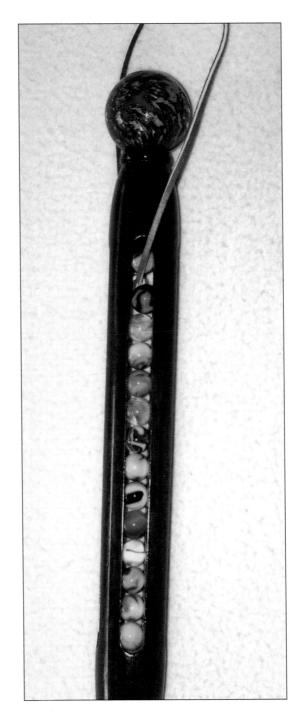

MARBLES ON STAMPS

KOREA NORTH   YUGOSLAVIA   BELGIUM   TANZANIA   SWEDEN   NEW ZEALAND

DOMINICAN REPUBLIC   MALAYSIA   MACAU   GREAT BRITAIN   NETHERLANDS ANTILLES   MOZAMBIQUE

SURINAME   SURINAME   KUWAIT   KUWAIT   EL SALVADOR   CHILE

Marbles on Stamps

Date of Issue	Country	Scott No.	Date of Issue	Country	Scott No.
11/21/67	Suriname	B138	5/9/89	Monaco	1682
1/10/77	Kuwait	684	7/31/89	Macau	597
11/7/78	Netherland Antilles	158	12/16/91	Lesotho	867
10/4/79	Chile	553	12/21/91	Mozambique	1165
7/21/80	Dominican Republic	832	1/28/92	Great Britain	1434
3/10/82	Dominica	756	5/2/96	North Korea PR	*
7/2/83	Argentina	B100	2/21/97	Singapore	777
10/16/84	El Salvador	1001	3/10/99	New Zealand	1579
11/23/87	Mongolia	1683	6/24/00	Malaysia	787-d
2/15/88	Tanzania	390	10/5/00	Sweden	400-b
4/29/89	Yugoslavia	1959	11/26/02	Israel	1498
5/8/89	Belgium	1312	5/27/03	Cayman Islands	877
			9/15/03	San Marino	1588

*North Korean People's Republic issued three Children Games stamps in set of two. Each set included a non-denomination "Cinderella" stamp showing boys playing marbles. Scott # is not listed because U.S. Treasury prohibits their purchase abroad and importation.

GLOSSARY OF TERMS

by William M. Parr

GLOSSARY OF TERMS

This glossary of terms presents accepted definitions of marbles and related terms.

AGATE. (1) Any marble made of agate, either handmade or machine made. Genuine antique handmade agate marbles are identified by the many minute facets that are the result of hand grinding. (2) A variegated stone, chalcedony, having its colors arranged in bands or stripes, blended in clouds, or showing moss-like forms. Most shades of earth colors occur, but the most common are alternations of reddish-browns with white. Agate can be dyed. *See also* CHALCEDONY.

AGATE GLASS. Glass made by blending two or more colored glasses, or by rolling transparent glass into powdered glass of various colors during the melting process. Any variegated glass made to simulate stone.

AGATE MARBLES. Marbles ground from agate, and historically prized for their durability and beauty. Also called carnelians. *See also* AGATE.

AGGIES. A common term used on the playgrounds of earlier times to refer to both glass and stone playing marbles of better quality or favored sort.

AKRO AGATE. A company established in Akron, Ohio, in 1911, for the purpose of making glass marbles and marble games. The name, Akro Agate, coined from the city name, became the trademark for all the company's glassware. Their symbol is a picture of a crow flying through the letter "A" with a marble in its beak, and clutching one in each claw. Circling the symbol was the legend "Shoot Straight as A Kro Flies." Akro is correctly pronounced "a crow."

ALLEYS. Derived from alleytors; prized shooters made of semiprecious minerals. *See also* AGGIES.

ANNEAL. The process of gradually reducing glass temperature, usually in an oven or lehr, for the purpose of balancing internal stresses throughout the glass, resulting in the prevention of fractures when the object reaches room temperature.

ANTIQUE. According to United States customs laws: an item, usually a work of art, furniture, or decorative object made at least one hundred years ago.

AVENTURINE. (1) Type of glass containing small articles of either copper (goldstone), chromic oxide (green aventurine) or ferric oxide (red aventurine) giving glass an intensely glittering appearance *(see LUTZ)*.

BANDED. Stripes of contrasting color curving pole to pole on handmade marbles—either on, in, or very near the surface.

BATCH. Mixture of raw materials, properly proportioned and mixed, ready for use in the manufacture of glass. Typical mixture includes: (1) silica sand (the relatively pure quartz base material); (2) soda or potash to lower the melting point; (3) lime to harden and make the metal easier to work; (4) lead for brilliance; (5) borax for greater hardness; (6) metallic oxides to clear and color; and (7) cullet to lower the melting temperature of the batch.

BENNINGTONS. Glazed pottery (crockery) marble, most often found in blues, browns, greens and mottled colors. *See also* CLAY, POTTERY.

BLACK SNAKE. Marble game using a series of holes, often played "for fair."

BLACK WIDOW. A color variety of machine made marbles having one bright red patch on opaque black glass.

BLOOD ALLEYS. An alley streaked or spotted with red. *See also* ALLEYS.

BLOODSTONE. Green chalcedony highlighted by red spots that resemble blood, and results from the oxidizing of the green material. Also known as heliotrope, it is considered a semiprecious stone. *See also* CHALCEDONY.

BLOWN GLASS. A glass object that is formed using blown air, as opposed to rolling, drawing, fusing, molding, etc. Marbles are not blown glass.

BOTTLE GLASS. Glass made from natural materials, no coloring agents added. Usually green or amber tint.

BOWLING. (1) Rolling the shot, on the ground, to hit a marble. (2) Any of several games in which balls are rolled on an outdoor green, or down an indoor alley, at an object or group of objects.

BOWLS. Also known as carpet balls (bowls). Stone porcelain or pottery spheres in various colors or patterns. About 3 inches in diameter, they are used in lawn, or small-scale indoor bowling games. *See also* BOWLING.

BRICK. A type of machine made red slag. The opaque base is the flat color of a dull red brick. The striping colors are black, clear, and white, each typically used sparingly. Called "Scotch Agate" by Ingram in *The Collector's Encyclopedia of Antique Marbles.*

BRUISED. The CONDITION of a marble that has received a visibly damaging blow, but no part has been chipped off. Sometimes does not reduce the value quite as much as chips. *See also* CONDITION.

BULLSEYE. (1) China marbles with concentric rings forming target design. (2) Agate marbles with the same "eye" design.

BUMBOOZER. A very large marble (1 inch and over) used as a bowling shooter. *See also* HOGGER.

CALCAREOUS. Stone having the nature of calcite or calcium carbonate, especially in hardness. For example, limestone and chalcedony.

CALCITE. A mineral formed of calcium carbonate crystallized in hexagonal form. It cleaves readily into rhombohedrons, and includes variations of chalk, limestone, dogtooth spar, Iceland spar, stalactites, stalagmites, and marble among others.

CANDLE SWIRL. A type of handmade swirl marble with latticinio center, usually with outer decoration of varying color bands running in a spiral from pole to pole. *See also* LATTICINIO.

CANDY SWIRL. A type of handmade swirl marble. Has a center that looks similar to Christmas candy. *See also* SOLID CORE, LOBED CORE.

CANE. A glass rod from which handmade marbles are fashioned. The rod is typically constructed layer upon layer of clear and contrasting colors.

CARNELIAN. (1) Colloquially, a marble made of agate. (2) A variety of chalcedony of a deep-red, flesh-red, or reddish-white color. Considered a semiprecious stone. *See also* AGATE, CHALCEDONY and QUARTZ.

CARPET BOWLS (BALLS). *See* BOWLS.

CASE GLASS. The glass covering on onionskins and swirls. Usually CRYSTAL, but transparent colors over crystal body glass can occur (*see* CRYSTAL).

CATSEYES. A machine made type introduced into the United States market from Japan about 1951.

CHALCEDONY. A translucent to opaque variety of quartz, most commonly pale tints of blue or gray, and waxlike luster. A semiprecious stone. Chalcedony of special or variegated colors is known as carnelian, agate, onyx, etc.

CHALKIES. Unglazed marbles made of gypsum, sometimes clay or limestone.

CHASIES. Marble game, usually with two players. Players alternate shooting at each other's marble. Also known as "follow-up" (Midwest).

CHINAS. Marbles made of porcelain. May be glazed or unglazed. Most often decorated with concentric rings of different colors, others are painted with flowers, fruit, trees, and other motif. Also called chinee, or chiny on the playground. See *also* PORCELAIN and POTTERY.

CHIPS. Pieces broken from the surface of a marble.

CLAMBROTH. A type of handmade glass marble. The body is one color, with evenly spaced, narrow color-strands running from pole to pole in the surface glass. May have sequences of two or more strand colors (also multicolored strands) occuring. The term CLAMBROTH is correctly reserved for this type when the body is milk glass (the color of clam broth).

CLAYS. Marbles made of clay which may or may not be colored or glazed. Common clays can be referred to as Commonys, or Commies.

CLEARS. A type of handmade glass marble. The body glass is transparent.

CLEARY. A type of machine made marble of undecorated transparent End-of-Day glass.

CLOUD MARBLES. A type of handmade End-of-Day marble resembling an onionskin. Has clouds of color rather than stretched lines of color. *See also* END-OF-DAY.

CLOUDY. Lacking clearness, brightness, or luster. When caused by surface wear it reduces the value and quality of the marble. *See also* CONDITION.

COLLECTIBLE. The worst marble condition expected in a collection. Badly damaged, but has some redeeming features. *See also* CONDITION.

COLLECTOR. One who gathers specimens for the purpose of study or ornament. Contrasts with accumulator in implying more careful selection that leads to enjoyment of the aesthetic values pursued...and the knowledge gained and shared in fellowship.

COMICS. Called "picture marbles" by Peltier Glass Co. when produced from 1926 through early 1930s. Twelve comic-strip character faces and names (Annie, Betty, Sandy, Ko Ko, Moon, Skeezix, Bimbo, Emma, Kayo, Smitty, Andy, Herbie) were printed on the marbles by a patented process that included a clear overglaze for permanence of the images. *See also* PICTURE MARBLES, PELTIER GLASS CO.

COMPATIBILITY. The mutual characteristics of two or more batches of glass that allow them to be fused together, and after proper cooling retain no stresses which will result in fractures. *See also* ANNEAL, BATCH.

CONDITION AND GRADING. The grading of condition is very subjective. Every collector has their own opinion and no two collectors will likely agree on the exact condition of a particular marble. The Marble

Collectors Society of America uses a descriptive grading system (Mint, Near Mint, Good, Collectible), which allows for some flexibility in grading. A numerical grading system based on a scale of 1 to 10 has also developed among marble collectors. The descriptions of each grading label used by the Society, along with the equivalent numerical grading is:

Mint: A marble that is in original condition. The surface is unmarked and undamaged. There may be some minor rubbing on the surface, however, the marble is just the way it came from the factory. (10.0 - 9.0)

Near Mint: A marble that has experienced minor usage. There may be evidence of some hit marks, usually tiny subsurface moons, pinprick chips, tiny flakes, or tiny bruises. The damage is inconsequential and does not detract from viewing the marble. If there is noticeable damage, and it is on only one side of the marble the other side is considered Mint. (8.9 - 8.0)

Good: A marble that has experienced minor usage. It will have numerous hit marks, subsurface moons, chips, flakes, or bruises. The core can still be clearly seen, but the marble has shows obvious use. If the damage is large or deep, and it is confined to one side the other side is considered Mint to Near Mint. (7.9 - 7.0)

Collectible: A marble that has experienced significant usage. Overall moons, chips, flakes, and bruises. The core is completely obscured in some spots. A collectible marble has served its purpose and been well used. Still, it is a placeholder in a collection until a better example replaces it. (6.9 - 0.0)

Any damage to the surface of a marble, no matter how slight, will affect its value. For a given amount of damage, the depreciation of value is much greater for machine made marbles than for handmade marbles. Even a small chip will effectively reduce the value of a machine made marble by more than half. Collectors tend to be more forgiving of damage to a handmade marble, this is likely because handmade marbles are more difficult to find.

The size of a marble is generally measured by its diameter in inches. Marble manufacturers utilize a sieve system of measuring. Using a device that measured marbles in 1/16 inch increments, the smallest opening that the marble would fall through was its size. Because of this method, the marbles classified as one size by a manufacturer could in fact vary by 3/64 inch. It is technically impossible to produce a handmade glass marble in sizes greater than approximately 2-1/2 inches in diameter because the marble would sag and deform during the annealing process due to its weight. However, different types of marbles are more common in some sizes than others. Machine made marbles are usually 1/2 inch to 3/4 inch. This is because marble tournament regulations set the size of the shooters to be between 1/2 inch and 3/4 inch and the size of the target marbles to be 5/8 inch. Again, the relative rarity of different sizes varies greatly from one type of marble to another.

CORKSCREW MARBLES. A type of machine made glass. The body glass may be opaque, translucent, or clear. Striping glass, of contrasting color or colors, forms one continuous line that spirals (corkscrews) from pole to pole making at least one full turn and never crossing. To date there is no known record of corkscrews made by any company other than Akro Agate. No corkscrew should ever be referred to as a swirl.

COTTAGE MARBLES. Machine mades not produced by a major manufacturer were produced by one of numerous cottage industries or "backyard glass shops" which were producing marbles during the 1920s and 1930s.

CRAZING. A network of fine cracks in the surface of a marble, can be caused by improper glazing of clays, or annealing of glass.

CROCKIES. Clay marbles in either solid or mottled colors, often glazed.

CRYSTAL. Clear, colorless glass; the body and case glass of most handmade marbles. Colorless as compared with colored transparent glass.

CULLET. Scraps of broken and waste glass to be re-melted. Cullet added to the batch lowers the melting point of the raw material. *See also* BATCH.

CUSTARD GLASS. Translucent yellow-green glass containing uranium trioxide as pigment which causes custard glass to be vividly florescent under black light. *See also* VASELINE GLASS.

CUTOFFS. The two rough spots on opposite poles of handmade marbles made from canes. Often mistakenly called "pontils," these rough spots show the marble was handmade (possibly in Germany before 1910). The presence of only one rough spot indicates that the marble may have been made from a gather on the end of a punty (pontil). The spot is then correctly called a pontil mark. Rough spots found (as they are occasionally) on machine made marbles indicate that some variable was out of adjustment in the manufacturing process (e.g., the glass may not have been hot enough to smooth out in the forming rollers). This is true even when referring to transition marbles that were hand-gathered on a pontil rod then machine-rounded on the forming rollers. *See also* PONTI, PUNTY.

DIAMETER. The length of a straight line through the center of an object. The size of a marble is measured by its greatest diameter.

DING. Minor damage to a marble caused by a blow, resulting in a small chip missing.

DIVIDED CORE. Type of handmade SWIRL marble having a core of two or more varicolored ribbons from pole to pole. Transparent glass at the marble's center is visible. *See also* SOLID CORE, DOUBLE RIBBON, SWIRL.

DOBIES. A term referring to clay or common marbles.

DOUBLE RIBBON. A variety of handmade ribbon core SWIRL having two ribbons, either matching or contrasting, parallel to each other which extend from pole to pole. *See also* SOLID CORE, RIBBON CORE, SWIRL.

DOUGH BABY. A CLAY marble term (of California origin); possibly a variation of "adobe," a clay for bricks.

DUBS. Knocking two or more marbles out of the ring with one shot.

DUCK. Object marbles to be shot at.

END-OF-CANE. A rare handmade marble that is actually a craftsman's imperfect. It comes from so near the end of the cane (perhaps the first marble made from that cane) that all of the intended colors were not included in the marble—usually an ugly marble. *See also* SWIRL, ONIONSKIN.

END-OF-DAY. Refers to a type and style of glass. Subclasses are panelled, cloud, onionskin, and Joseph's Coat; all of which may have one or two pontils.

ENGLISH SWIRLS. Vibrant brightly colored marbles where the origin is close to the surface. Refers to both swirls and End-of-Day marbles with the vivid colors of red, yellow, orange, and green.

EXCELLENT. An obscure term when referring to condition of a marble. Mint is less subjective, and has been recognized to describe the best condition of a marble that remains undamaged but not in its original container. *See also* MINT, CONDITION.

FEN. Used as a ritual call by children, especially in certain games (as marbles) to prevent certain actions by an opponent or teammate, or to exempt the first caller from a task or action. Meant to prevent (e.g., fen dubs) a player, upon hitting two marbles in one shot, from taking both.

FIRE POLISH. (1) The natural process gloss left on a marble by the heat used in manufacturing. (2) The polish resulting from subjecting a preheated marble to direct flame or radiant heat. Not a recommended procedure for novices.

FLINT. (1) A somewhat impure quartz that ranges in color from light gray to brown-black. Handmade flint marbles do exist. (2) Crystal glass, so called because a fine antique British glass was originally made by substituting pulverized flint for silica sand. *See also* BATCH.

FOR FAIR. Playing so as to return to the former owner all marbles won during the game.

FOR KEEPS. Playing without returning opponent's marbles.

FUDGING. Easing the hand over ring line when in the act of shooting. Forbidden in tournament play. Term replaces "cheating" if opponent is a big kid.

FURNACE. Any of various ovens used for melting the glass batch. A kiln.

GATHER. A portion of molten glass on a pontil. *See also* METAL, PUNTY, PONTIL.

GENERAL GRANT GAME. An early form of the board game "Solitare." This game board was round and had a handpainted silhouette of the bust of Grant on the surface of the board.

GERMAN SWIRL. Handmade glass marbles made in Germany. Most were made before 1910.

GLASS. An amorphous (uncrystallized) substance consisting ordinarily of a silica (as sand), an alkali (as potash or soda), and some other alkali (as lime or lead oxide) fused together. Various colors are imparted by the addition of metallic oxides. *See also* BATCH, METAL.

GLAZE. The vitreous (glass) coating on china and pottery marbles that imparts the smooth glossy finish. Applied as either liquid or powder (flour glaze) the marbles are again heated and ANNEALED. Dull pottery marbles are unglazed, or glaze has lost its sheen through use or abuse. COMICS received a flour glaze after the picture was applied. *See also* COMICS.

GLORY HOLE. An opening into the furnace or kiln. Used for reheating the gather of glass (the marble) when making a piece on a punty. *See also* PONTIL.

GOLDSTONE. (1) Common name for synthetic aventurine substitute. A type of glass containing fine particles of copper that sparkle. *See also* AVENTURINE.

GOOD. Third from best CONDITION on a scale of four. *See also* CONDITION.

GOOSEBERRY. A transparent glass marble with uniform strands of glass close to the surface.

GRANITE. Marbles made of granite, a hard igneous rock that takes a high polish.

GROUND. Refers to repairing a marble when considerable outer glass must be removed. If done by an expert, by hand, pontil marks may possibly be saved. When done on a sphere grinder, pontil marks are removed. When done in rock tumbler the marble is usually ruined.

HANDMADE. Marbles made without use of machines, the exception being those held in the fingers against a power driven grinding wheel (e.g., agates made before 1910). Few handmade marbles of any sort can be expected to be perfect spheres; clay, pottery and china types are most out-of-round.

HISTING. Raising the hand from the ground while in the act of shooting. Not allowed in tournament play. The cause of many blackened eyes.

HOGGER. Any marble larger than 7/8 inch, and typically approximately 1 inch. Commonly, and misleadingly, called "shooter" size. Very few marbles were won with one of those big targets, and are nearly impossible to shoot properly off the knuckle.

HUNCHING. Moving the hand forward while shooting over the ring line. Not allowed in tournament play. Also known as poking (Midwest).

IMMIE. A glass machine made marble streaked with color.

INDIAN SWIRL. Handmade marble of dark base glass with colorful strands applied to the surface. Base glass may be opaque, semi-opaque, or translucent. Usually does not have a casing layer of glass.

INGOT. Rough balls of glass intended for use in modern, automatically fed glass furnaces and insulation manufacture. Some have green tint, but most have orange-peel surface. Can often be found along railroad tracks, or in jars of marbles offered at flea markets.

IRIDESCENCE. The rainbow-like display of shifting colors exhibited by thin films such as oil on water. Iridescence of carnival glass marbles is produced by the process of fuming (i.e., spraying the hot glass with an iridizing solution of metallic salts in diluted hydrochloric acid). Example: a combination of tin, chlorine, and zinc produces opalescent foggy white over most glass colors; a combination of tin and iron salts produces blue, green, and silver over most glass. *See also* OPALESCENT GLASS.

JADES. Marbles made of the gemstone jade, usually green.

JASPERS. (1) Marbles made of jasper, a form of CHALCEDONY. (2) Playground name for LINED CROCKERY marbles.

JOSEPH'S COAT. An End-of-Day or Swirl type marble having colorful strands all around the marble. Usually with one to four black or dark blue strands mixed in.

KABOLA. Oversized marble of jawbreaker size. *See also* HOGGER.

KILN. Any of various ovens, furnaces, used for the purpose of melting the glass batch, typically of brick construction ceramic fiber lined, and in the larger sizes, heated with natural gas. *See also* LEHR, ANNEAL.

KLICKERS. Old name for marbles made of agate and semiprecious stone, mentioned by Paul Baumann in *Collecting Antique Marbles*, and still currently in use in Europe.

KNUCKLES DOWN. To rest one or more of one's knuckles on the ground while shooting. A general term denoting the correct form for marble shooting. The marble should rest against the ball of the first finger rather than in the crook.

LAG. To pitch or shoot at a mark, marble, hole or other target. In some areas (Midwest) to pitch as distinguished from shoot.

LAG LINE. A straight line tangent to the ring in tournament play.

LAGGING. The act of tossing or shooting from the pitching line. Whoever comes closest to the lag line, without going over it, shoots first.

LATTICINIO. (1) Filigree glass of Venetian invention. Appears to have spiraling, crossing, or interlacing fine opaque threads, in crystal base. (2) A type of handmade SWIRL marble with filigree center core.

LATTICINIO CORE. Innermost part of SWIRL made of latticinio glass (also called filigree, lace, or net core). Marbles commonly have colorful outer decoration spiraling from pole to pole. *See also* CANDLE SWIRL, SWIRL.

LEHR. An oven in which glassware is annealed, typically fitted with a continuous belt feed. *See also* ANNEAL, KILN.

LINED CROCKERY. A type of pottery marble made from two or more colors of clay, which produce random areas of sharp contrast. Also called JASPERS. *See also* POTTERY.

LOBED. One of the types of cores in a marble. Occurs in SOLID CORE SWIRLS and END-OF-DAY marbles.

LOBED CORE. A type of SOLID CORE which has a cross-sectional shape of a cog wheel, a clover leaf, or other repeated pattern of flutes, ribs, vanes, or grooves. Solid cores show a crystal center when sawed in half. If the clear center is visible the marble's value is reduced. Solid cores are not to be confused with Peltier catseye machine mades. *See also* CANDY SWIRL, SINGLE RIBBON, DIVIDED CORE, SOLID CORE.

LOFTING. The act of shooting a marble through the air in an arc to hit another marble, or other target. Sometimes called popping.

LUTZ. A handmade glass marble containing aventurine. This type occurs in most designs of SWIRLS. *See also* AVENTURINE.

MACHINE MADES. Marbles commercially produced by machine.

MARBLE SHEARS. The tool used to hold, form, and cut a handmade marble as it is being made from the hot cane. Similar to tongs or sheep shears, but having a cup on one side and a blade on the other.

MARBLES. Marbles are little balls made of hard substances (as stone, glass, porcelain, clay, metal, etc.) typically from 5/8 inch to 2 inches in diameter. Decorative marbles are as large as 3 inches and as small as 1/4 inch.

MARVING. The controlled forming of viscous glass on a flat metal table (a marver, it was formerly made of polished marble). The technique is used in manufacturing handmade marbles. Grooved marvers hold colored glass that becomes the decorative ribbons and strands in SWIRLS.

METAL. Molten (viscous) glass. *See also* GLASS.

M.I.B. The acronym for Mint-in-Box refers to original marbles, in their original box, in original condition. *See also* CONDITION, MINT, NEAR MINT.

MIBS. The game of marbles; represents shortening of the word marbles.

MICA. (1) Mineral silicates that cleave into thin sheets—usually reflective, often silvery (most other colors occur). (2) The type of handmade glass marbles a majority of which are Clears with flecks of mica interspersed within the marble. Mica was introduced intentionally into some onionskins, and accidentally intruded into most other handmades as craftsman's defects. *See also* CLEARS.

MIGGLES. Common playing marble; term usually referred to small clays. Also called Migs. *See also* COMMIES, COMMONIES.

MILKIES. Translucent white glass marbles, either handmade or machine made.

MINT. Established by long usage as the standard term meaning the original undamaged condition. *See also* CONDITION.

MOON AGGIES. Marbles made of CARNELIAN. So called because a blow or hit usually produces a moon or crescent shape fracture inward from the surface rather than a chip. When soaked in mineral oil or lard the moon may become very difficult to detect. *See also* AGATE.

MOONIES. (1) Opalescent marbles. (2) Name given by Peltier Glass Co. to their harvest moon colored opalescent marble. *See also* OPALESCENT GLASS.

MOSS AGATE. Variety of agate having inclusions of brown, black, or green moss-like shapes. Realistic tree like inclusions occur. *See also AGATE.*

NEAR-MINT. Refers to condition of a marble. Accepted by usage as next best grade. *See also* CONDITION.

ONIONSKIN. A type of End-of-Day handmade glass marble. Onionskins appear to be colorful opaque spheres with a covering of case glass, but in fact, a thin layer of color covers a large transparent center. Onionskins are made from canes. Some canes were stretched very little, leaving the colors in blotches. Other canes were stretched enough to make the col-

ors appear as long streaks extending from pole to pole. The more typical style of onionskin has a thin layer of white and/or yellow covering the clear base glass and forming a background for the contrasting colors. *See also* END-OF-DAY.

ONYX. (1) Quartz in parallel layers of different colors. *See also* CHALCEDONY. (2) Onyx seems to have been a catch-all term in early catalogs offering machine made glass marbles.

OPALESCENT GLASS. Translucent glass that exhibits a milky iridescence like the gemstone opal. The image of an incandescent light filament transmitted through a sheet of opalescent glass appears as a red outline. Marbles made of opalescent glass "fire" red/yellow in the center when held up to incandescent light or the sun. Not to be confused with the iridescence of carnival glass, which is a surface feature. *See also* IRIDESCENT.

OPAQUE. (1) Impervious to the rays of light; neither transparent nor translucent. (2) A type of handmade glass marble made of opaque glass, which may be decorated with bands extending from pole to pole. The BANDED OPAQUE family, like the BANDED CLEAR family has a more formal controlled, precise, prim pattern of color arrangement than the brushed-on-look of the INDIAN family. *See also* INDIAN SWIRL.

PEE WEE. Refers to a marble with 1/2 inch or smaller maximum diameter.

PEE DAB. A small clay marble (term used in Georgia, pronounced PEE DAD in parts of midwest). A marble of such little value as to be excluded from most games played "for keeps," or by the older boys.

PELTIER GLASS COMPANY. Founded in Ottawa, Illinois, in 1886, Peltier Glass is the oldest continuously producing glass company in the United States. Peltier has made game marbles since 1920, and continues today. Best known among collectors for making COMICS, Peltier has also created some of the most desirable machine made marbles. *See also* COMIC and PICTURE MARBLES.

PEPPERMINT SWIRL. A type of handmade glass marble. Easily identified because it looks like a ball of peppermint candy, usually red, white, and blue. Reportedly a United States centennial commemorative marble when it contains mica flakes in the blue banding. Construction is similar to an ONIONSKIN.

PICTURE MARBLES. The machine made marbles produced by Peltier Glass Co. using a complicated process patented by Geo. W. Angerstein. Most carried a picture of a popular comic strip character, others carried advertising. *See also* GLAZE, COMIC MARBLES, PELTIER.

PITCH LINE. A straight line tangent to the ring, directly opposite and parallel to the lag line in the game of ringer. *See also* LAG LINE.

POLE. Refers to the two opposite points on a handmade marble where the decorations terminate, and cut-off marks should be found. *See also* CUT-OFF, PUNTY.

POLISHING. Removal of haze from the surface of a marble. When done properly does not reduce value of the marble, and can greatly increase its beauty. Performed in a way (similar to grinding) where the polishing compound is applied to a cotton buffer.

PONTIL. A long, solid steel rod. A device used to make the gather, to turn the gather while forming the marble, to finish and to fire polish. Also called a punty. *See also* PUNTY.

PONTIL MARK. A rough mark left on one or both poles of a handmade marble where the marble was sheared off the rod or the end of the punty. A cut off mark left on the marble.

POOR. Refers to condition of a marble. Marble has serious damage, chips, and/or cloudy surface. *See also* CONDITION.

POPEYES. A variety of machine made corkscrew made to include one color of glass in addition to yellow, white, and colorless. Typical colors are red, blue, or purple. The colors are distinctive in being groups of fine strands or threads. Made by Akro Agate in the 1950s, called "Popeyes" because the comic strip character appeared on original promotional packaging. Corkscrews of similar design, but with different colors, were usually not packaged in Popeye boxes. *See also* CORKSCREWS.

PORCELAIN. A hard, fine-grained, non-porous, and most often translucent white ceramic ware that consists primarily of kaolin, quartz, and feldspar. It is fired at high temperature, and does not absorb water. *See also* CHINAS.

POTSIES. Name for the game of ringer. Also called dubs.

POTTERY. Earthenware as distinguished from porcelain, stoneware, brick, and tile. *See also* BENNINGTONS.

PUNTY. An iron or steel rod used to fashion hot glass which is attached by a rod of glass first gathered on the punty. Where detached from the glass it leaves a rough spot.

PURIE. Small, clear, colorful machine made glass marbles. *See also* CLEARY.

QUARTZ. (1) The most common of all solid minerals, it is a form of silica (silicon dioxide) having hexagonal crystals. Typically colorless, but naturally occurring in many colors. (2) Quartz-laden sand is the largest ingredient in making glass. *See also* BATCH.

RIBBON CORE. A rare type of handmade SWIRL having one flat ribbon which spirals through the center from pole to pole. See SWIRL, SPIRAL, SINGLE RIBBON SWIRL, DOUBLE RIBBON, DIVIDED CORE.

RING TAW (RINGER). A game in which marbles are placed in a ring marked on the ground, and shot at, with player's taw, from the outer edge of the ring. The player knocking the most marbles from the ring is the winner.

ROSE QUARTZ. (1) A rose-red to pink variety of the mineral quartz.

SEED BUBBLES. Tiny air bubbles in old glass. Deliberately placed seed bubbles in contemporary handmade marbles.

SEEDY GLASS. Glass containing many small gaseous inclusions (bubbles), usually introduced intentionally into base glass of both handmade and machine made marbles to create visual texture. *See also* SWIRL MARBLES.

SHOOTER. (1) In play, the marble shot from the hand. Maximum size allowed in tournament play is 3/4 inch. (2) Mechanical device (usually patented) for propelling a marble. *See also* HOGGER.

SINGLE PONTIL. Term for handmade marbles having only one cutoff mark; includes CLOUDS, some MICAS, SLAGS, and miscellaneous oddities.

SINGLE RIBBON. A variety of handmade SWIRL with a flat ribbon shaped core, either thick or thin. *See also* RIBBON CORE and SOLID CORE.

SIZE. Usually measured with vernier calipers (brass or plastic), hand-made marble size is the longest diameter. Machine made marbles are sized as follows:

7/16 inch	0000	1/16 inch	1	15/16 inch	5
1/2 inch	000	3/4 inch	2	1 inch	6
1/16 inch	00	13/16 inch	3	1-1/16 inch	7
5/8 inch	0	7/8 inch	4	1-1/8 inch	8

SLAG. Types of marbles made of slag glass, either handmade or machine made.

SLAG GLASS. (1) A glass that simulates the patternless mixture of hues found in natural variegated stone marble and agate. Slag glass may be transparent as well as opaque. Any marbled glass blended without predetermined pattern—variegated. (2) The glasslike wastes from metal smelting furnaces. *See also* CARNELIAN.

SLIP. (1) Misplay when marble falls from the hand. Player shoots over. (2) Player who drops the marble must call "slips" before Opponent calls "no slips" or looses the turn to shoot over (playgrounds in Midwest). (3) The soupy mixture of clay used to cast sulfide figures. *See also* SULFIDES.

SNOOGER. A near miss in a game of marbles.

SODA LIME GLASS. Glass made from silica, soda, and lime. See BATCH.

SOLID CORE. A type of handmade glass SWIRL marble having a center decoration that appears to be a solid geometric shape extending from pole to pole. The core is typically white, sometimes yellow, rarely other colors, and commonly decorated with colored strands or ribbons. Outer decorative lines of color are usually present near the marble's surface. *See also* CANDY SWIRL, RIBBON CORE SWIRL, SPIRAL.

SOLITAIRE. Popular marble game of the 19th century. Played by one player using a round board (General Grant Game Board) incised with thirty-three round depressions, the object of the game is to remove each jumped marble (as in the game of checkers, draughts) so that one marble remains resting in the center spot on the board. *See also* GENERAL GRANT GAME BOARD.

SPANNERS. A shooting distance. The measurement between the tip of the thumb to the tip of the middle finger when stretched apart.

SPIRAL. Winding, curving, coiling, or circling around a center or pole and more or less receding (or approaching) it. The path of the decorations of most swirl marbles. Term sometimes applied to a SWIRL. *See also* SWIRL.

STEELY. (1) A hollow marble made of steel (sometimes brass) that can be identified by light weight and a "+" on one side where the thin metal meets, made in 1-1/16 inch and 5/8 inch sizes. (2) Common name given to ball bearings.

STICK. A shooter's marble (stops) inside the ring after knocking a target marble out of the ring. The player may continue to shoot as long as the shooter sticks inside the ring.

STRIA. Elongated imperfections in glass. May be bubbles or caused by unequal density of glasses used. Stria cause variation in intensity of hues, as in stained glass windows. *See also* BATCH, ANNEAL, COMPATIBILITY.

SULFIDE MARBLES. A type of handmade marble produced of transparent glass, and containing one or more sulfide (clay) figures of persons, animals, toys, numerals, or other objects. Sulfide marbles made of colored transparent glass, with multiple figures, or with painted sulfide objects occur. (Also spelled sulphide.)

SULFIDES. Ceramic objects cast or molded of china clay and supersilicate of potash for inclusion in marbles, and other glassware. (Also spelled sulphide.)

SWIRL. (1) A whirling motion, or something characterized by such a motion; whirl, curve, or twist around a point or line. (2) A type of HANDMADE glass marble with ribbons or strands of colored glass twisting around the inside axis. *See also* SPIRAL, LATTICINIO, SINGLE RIBBON, SOLID CORE SWIRL.

TAWS. (1) Term derived from alleytor; prized shooter made of semiprecious minerals. (2) Another name for shooter. (3) The line or other agreed upon starting point of a game of marbles (Midwest).

THRIBS. Term refers to three marbles, and usually used in the ritual call "fen thribs," meaning to prevent an opponent who has hit three marbles from taking more than one.

TIGEREYE. A mineral marble, usually brown, with bright reflecting inside sheen bands, which are usually golden, but may be red or purple. The reflection is caused by asbestos fibers naturally enclosed in a base of quartz.

TWO FERS. Marbles originally priced two for one cent. Anything cheap.

VASELINE. (1) Transparent glass that shifts between yellow and green in sun light, and is fluorescent green under black light. Called Vaseline because it resembles the petroleum jelly product. Vaseline glass contains the coloring agent uranium trioxide, which produces the brilliant florescence under high intensity ultraviolet (black) light, and which activates radiation detection devices. (2) Marbles made of Vaseline glass.

WET MINT. Referring to CONDITION of a marble. Wet mint look can be applied to the surface of a marble with a coating of liquid acrylic floor wax. *See also* CONDITION, MINT, POLISH.

LIST OF MARBLE CLUBS

A complete list of active clubs at the time of publication is listed below.

Badger Marble Club
P.O. Box 194, Waunakee, WI 53597
Dennis Lancaster, Sec. 419-814-0233

Blue Ridge Marble Club
Roger Dowdy, 3410 Plymouth Place, Lynchburg, VA 24503
Shows held in March and September (both in Lynchburg, VA)
Periodic newsletter

Blue Ridge Marble Club - Southwest Virginia Chapter
Junior Stoots, 101 McArthur Street, Galax, VA 24333

Buckeye Marble Club
Scott Strasburger, P.O. Box 6, Franklin OH 45005
Shows held in February (New Philadelphia, PA) and August (Columbus, OH)
Periodic newsletter

Canadian Marble Collectors Association
George Hoy, RR #1 Dunnganon, Ontario Canada
Non - IRO
Craig Gamache, 10B Murdock Street, Georgetown, Ontario, Canada L7G 3L6

Great Plains Marble Club
c/o Steve Campbell, 508 Sixth St., Glenwood, IA 51534, 712-527-9162

Maine Marble Collectors
c/o Mickie Pasanen, 47 Gorham Rd., Gorham, ME 04038, 207-839-4726

Marble Collectors Society of America
Stanley Block, P.O. Box 222, Trumbull, CT 06611
Quarterly newsletter. Other publications.

Marble Collectors Unlimited
Beverly Brule, P.O. Box 206, Northboro, MA 05132

Show held in June (Amana, IA)
Periodic newsletter

Midwest Marble Collectors
3 Mallard Lane, St. Paul, MN 55127
Kenneth Royer, Treas., 612-484-7683

National Marble Club of America
Jim Ridpath, 440 Eaton Road, Drexel Hill, PA 19026
Periodic newsletter

Oklahoma Marble Collectors
c/o Neil or Debbie Thacker, 16328 South Peoria, Bixby, OK 74008 918-322-9221

Sea-Tac Marble Club
Larry Van Dyke, P.O. Box 793, Monroe, WA 98272
Shows in May (Denver, CO) March (Seattle, WA), June (Santa Cruz, CA) and November (Las Vegas, NV)
Periodic newsletter

South Jersey Marble Collectors
c/o Joseph C. Brauner, Jr., 7709 Raymond Dr., Millville, NJ 08332, 609-785-1862

Southern California Marble Collectors Society
Sherry Ellis, P.O. Box 6913, San Pedro, CA 90734
Show held in January (Los Angeles, CA)

Suncoast Marble Collectors Society
Catherine Kortvely, P.O. Box 60213, St. Petersburg, FL 22784
Show held in February (Clearwater, FL)
Periodic newsletter

Texas Marble Collectors
Michael Moreland, 214-296-6419
John Tags, 210-620-0219

Tri-State Marble Collectors Club
David French, P.O. Box 18924, Fairfield, OH 45018
Show held in October

BIBLIOGRAPHY

This bibliography is excerpted from the Marble Collectors Society of America's Library Bibliography, as compiled by James H. Davis.

Ace, Goodman. "Top of My Head: The Art of Knuckling Down." *Saturday Review*, 29 January 1972: 8.

"The Aesthetic of the Mib." *Esquire*, August 1968: 86-87.

Allen, Shirley. "Windy." *The Game of Marbles*. 1953. Paden City, West Virginia: Marble King, Inc., 1967.

Alvis, Carmen. "The Marbles Just Keep Rolling Out of City Plant." *Parkersburg (WV) Sentinel*, 24 March, 1984: 11.

"Anybody Remember How to Play Marbles?" *Changing Times*, March 1958: 45-46.

Armstrong, Joan. "She Wants All the Marbles." *News-Gazette* (Champaign, Illinois), 19 Oct. 1981: A1, A5.

Avedon, Elliot M., and Brian Sutton-Smith, eds. *The Study of Games*. New York: Wiley, 1971: "Folklore Source": 159-66 (65). "Historical Sources": 121-27 (22).

Barrett, Marilyn. *Aggies, Immies, Shooters and Swirls: The Magical World of Marbles*. Little, Brown and Company, 1994.

Batchelor, Denzil. "Marbles: On Good Friday They Are Playing for the British Championship." *Leader Magazine* (U.K.), 20 April 1946: 13-15.

Baumann, Paul. *Collecting Antique Marbles*. Wallace Homestead Book Co., 1991.

Block, Robert. *Marbles: Identification and Price Guide*. Atglen, Pennsylvania: Schiffer Publishing, Ltd., 1996, 1998.

Block, Stanley. "Marbles - Playing for Fun and For Keeps." *The Encyclopedia of Collectibles - Lalique to 7° Marbles*. Time-Life Publications, 1983.

Botermans, Jack, Tony Burret, Pieter van Delft, and Carla van Splunteren. "Marbles." *The World of Games*. New York: Facts on File, 1989: 5, 7, 182, 212-13.

Brunvand, Jan Harold. ("Marble Terms.") *The Study of American Folklore*. New York: Norton, 1968; 230.

Bullard, M. Kenyon. "Marbles: An Investigation of the Relationship between Marble Games and Other Aspects of Life in Belize." *Journal Of American Folklore* 88 (Oct.-Dec. 1975): 393-401.

Canova, Enrique C. "West Virginia: Treasure Chest of Industry." NATIONAL GEOGRAPHIC, Aug. 1940: 141-84 (183 84, pl. vi).

Carskadden, Jeff, and Mark Randall. "The Christensen Agate Company, Cambridge, Ohio—1927-1933." *Muskingum Annals* 4 (Zanesville, OH; 1987): 48-52.

Carksadden, Jeff, Richard Gartley, and Elizabeth Reeb. "Marble Making and Marble Playing in Eastern Ohio: The Significance of Ceramic, Stone, and Glass Marbles in Historic Archaeology." Proc. of the Symposium on Ohio Valley Urban and Historic Archaeology 3 (1985): 86-96.

Castle, Larry, and Marlowe Peterson. *The Guide to Machine-Made Marbles*. Utah Marble Connection Inc.: 1995.

Chan, Mei-Mei. "Young Sharpshooters Go for All the Marbles." *USA Today*, 25 June 1984: D1.

Cahpin, Dwight. "He'll Take All Comers." *San Francisco Examiner*, 4 February 1985: C1.

Chestney, Linda. "Collectibles: Marbles." *New Hampshire Profiles*, April 1984: 29-32, 37, 48-49 (30, 48).

"Children Drop Video Games for Marbles." *Hour* (Norwalk, Connecticut), 24 July 1986: 20.

Childress, William. "How I Lost My Marbles." *Ford Times*, April 1989: 12-17.

Clark, F. C. *Marbles As Played In Weald Of Kent 1800-1900*. Sandhurst, Kent, England: Clark, 1962.

Combes, Abbot. "Congress, Media, Marbles." *Washington Star*, 26 May 1976: E1, E3.

Connor, Helen. "Professor's Hobby 'Marble-ous.' "*Indianapolis Star*, 3 January 1982, sec. 5:1-2.

Cowley, Susan Cheever. "Newsmaker (First Congressional Marbles Tournament)." *Newsweek*, 7 June 1976: 44.

DiBacco, Thomas V. "Childhood's Marble-ous Training Ground." *Wall Street Journal*, 16 June 1988: 22.

Ferrell, W. C. "Shootin' Marbles." Poem and Norman Rockwell's "Marble Champion" ("Knuckles Down") *Ideals*, 6 August 1964: 12-13.

Ferretti, Fred. "Marbles: The Toys For Tight Budgets." *New York Times*, 4 June 1980: C1, C13.

Forbes, Malcom S. "Do Kids Still Play Marbles?" *Forbes*, 13 September 1982: 20.

Freeman, Ruth and Larry Freeman. "Balls, Marbles and

Play-Ball." *Cavalcade Of Toys*. New York: Century House, 1942; 112-13, 116.

Frey, Robert L. "Marbles + Golf = Marble Golf." *Recreation*, March 1931: 658, 690-91.

Garland, Robert. "That's Marbles, Son." *Saturday Evening Post*, 13 July 1946: 69.

Gildea, William. "Marbles: They Knelt to Conquer." *Washington Post*, 13 June 1974: B1, B3.

Gold, Anita. "Antiques: Shows, Auctions, Clubs Come into Play for Toy Collectors." *Chicago Tribune*, 13 June 1986, sec 7: 53.

Grunfeld, Frederic V., ed. "Marbles." *Games Of The World*. New York: Holt, 1975; 158-60.

Hopper, Lynn. "Hoosier Antiques and Collectibles: Marbles Among Collecting's Small but Pricey Treasures." *Indianapolis Star*, 31 May 1987: 9G.

Howard, Dorothy. "Marbles." *Dorothy's World: Childhood In Sabine Bottom* (1902-1910). Englewood Cliffs, New Jersey: Prentice, 1977; 218-19.

Howe, Bea. "The Charm of Old Marbles." *Country Life*, 11 December 1969: 1593.

Howe, Jennifer. "Ante Up: How to Play a Round of Marbles." *Kansas City Star*, 15 June 1991: E1, E7.

Huffer, Lloyd, and Chris Huffer. "Marbles: Today's Game Is Collecting." *Antiques And The Arts Weekly*, 11 May 1990: 1, 108-10.

Johnson, Bruce. "Knock on Wood: Marbles May Prevent Tung Oil Hardening in Its Container." *Antiqueweek*, 13, July 1987: 16.

Johnson, Owen. "In Marble Time: The Ruling Passion of the Boy, Small and Large, Near and Far, When the Warm Days of Springtime Come." *Collier's*, 15 April 1911: 23, 42.

Lidz, Franz. "Spotlight: Here's a Man Who Has All of His Marbles—Maybe Some of Yours, Too." *Sports Illustrated*, 3 December 1984: 7.

Loeper, John J. "A Pocketful of Marbles." *The Shop On High Street; The Toys And Games Of Early America*. New York: Atheneum, 1978: 73-76.

Looney, Douglas S. "Nostalgia and Yawns Meet in a Clash of Taws and Greenies." *National Observer*, 21 June 1971: 14.

Louis, Sally B. "Playing for Keeps: Collecting Antique Marbles." *New York-Pennsylvania Collector*, December 1985: 1B-2B, 4B.

"Marble Society Begins 14th Year." *Antiques and Arts Weekly*, 25 November 1988: 37.

"Marble Society Produces Video." *American Collector's Journal*, September 1987: 4.

"Marbles." *New York Times Magazine*, 20 July 1941: 2.

"Marbles." *Saturday Review*, 26 July 1884: 107-08.

McClinton, Katherine Morrison. "Marbles." *Antiques Of American Childhood*. New York: Barmahall, 1970; 207-09.

Metzerott, Mary. "Notes on Marble History." *Hobbies*, November 1941: 56-57.

Milberg, Alan. "Marbles." *Street Games*. New York: McGraw, 1976: 92-96.

Mustain, Nellie M. "Marbles." *A Complete Library Of Entertainment, Amusement, Instruction For Every Occasion*. New York: Martin, 1903: 216.

Panati, Charles. "Marbles: 3000 B.C., Egypt." *Extraordinary Origins Of Everyday Things*. New York: Perrenial-Harper, 1987: 368-69.

Proctor, John. "Marble King." *Family Circle*, 23 June 1939; 1, 14-15.

Randall, Mark E. "Early Marbles." *Historical Archaeology* 5 (1971): 102-05.

Randall, Mark E., and Dennis Webb. *Greenberg's Guide To Marbles*. Sykeville, Maryland: Greenberg, 1988.

Remas, Michael. "Knuckling Down to Marbles." *Christian Science Monitor*, 11 Oct. 1969: 15.

Robinson, Grady Jim. "Nostalgia: 'Twas a Sad Day When the Author Lost All His Marbles." *Sports Illustrated*, 16 November 1981: 110, 112.

Rubenstein, Steven. "It's a Great Marble, But It's Still a Marble." *San Francisco Chronicle*, 21 December 1990: E22.

Runyan, Cathy. *Knuckles Down! A Guide to Marble Play*. Right Brain Publishing Co.

Soble, Ronald L. "Your Collectibles: Losing His Marbles to Highest Bidder." *Los Angeles Times*, 20 March 1986, sec. 5: 20.

Spendlove, Earl. "He Has All His Marbles." *Rock And Gem*, June 1991: 56-59, 84.

Steadham, Edward. "Enthusiast from Trumbull Shoots for World's Best Marble Collection." *Bridgeport Post*, 26 November 1983: 15.

Vinton, Iris. "Beans, Peas and Marbles as Universal Playthings." *The Folkways Omnibus Of Children's Games*. Harrisburg, Pennsylvania: Stackpole, 1970; 112-120.

Vogel, Carol. "Crossing Over." *New York Times Magazine*, 5 May 1985: 80-81.

Walker, Stanley. "The Game of Marbles." *Good Housekeeping*, March 1945: 25, 135-37.

Watson, Henry D. "Antique Marbles of Stone, Pottery and Glass." AMERICAN COLLECTOR, July 1942: 6- 7, 15.

Webb, Dennis. *Greenburg's Guide to Marbles*. Second Edition. Greenberg Publishing Co.: 1994.

INDEX